Drew Provan

iPad

8th edition
covers all models of iPad with iOS 12
(including iPad mini and iPad Pro)

In easy steps is an imprint of In Easy Steps Limited
16 Hamilton Terrace · Holly Walk · Leamington Spa
Warwickshire · United Kingdom · CV32 4LY
www.ineasysteps.com

Eighth Edition

In Easy Steps Limited supports The Forest Stewardship Council (FSC),
the leading international forest certification organisation. All our titles
that are printed on Greenpeace approved FSC certified paper carry the
FSC logo.

MIX
Paper from
responsible sources
FSC
www.fsc.org   FSC® C020837

Rotherham MBC	
B54 029 730 6	
Askews & Holts	07-Jan-2019
004.1675	£10.99
SWI	

Printed and bound in the United Kingdom

ISBN 978-1-84078-816-7

Contents

1 Welcome to Your New iPad

The iPad is a high-quality multimedia tablet. Its rich graphics and seamless integration with the pre-installed apps make it perfect for work and play. Most tasks requiring a laptop can be carried out on the iPad (with its iOS 12 operating system), which is light, power-efficient, quickly-on and incredibly intuitive to use. It also has an huge number of third-party apps to expand its already impressive capabilities and performance.

Welcome to the iPad!

Congratulations on buying an iPad; a sophisticated multimedia tablet computer capable of playing music, dealing with emails, browsing the web, organizing your calendar and thousands of other applications! Or maybe you haven't bought an iPad yet, but are considering doing so. Let's look at what you can use the iPad for:

- Listening to music.

- Browsing the web.

- Emails, contacts and calendars.

- Social networking.

- Taking photos.

- Recording and watching videos.

- Reading ebooks.

- FaceTime video chats, playing games, and much more.

Will it replace my laptop?

In some cases, yes; particularly with the iPad Pro, which is capable of significant productivity tasks and also has its own physical keyboard (sold separately). If you mainly do web browsing, check emails and use social networking apps then the iPad or iPad mini can easily replace your laptop. If, on the other hand, you use your laptop to generate PowerPoint slides or create complex documents, then the iPad Pro may be a better option in terms of a replacement device.

What's missing from the iPad?

There are features found on laptops and desktops that are missing from the iPad. At present there is no:

- **SD photo card slot**. If you want to download photos from a SD card, a separate adapter is required.

- **USB slots**. Although iPads do not have any USB slots, USB devices can be connected with a separate USB adapter.

- **A sophisticated file management system**. The Files app can be used to manage some files, but there is not the same kind of file hierarchy as found on a laptop or desktop computer.

Beware

Depending on your needs, the iPad may not be a laptop replacement. Assess your needs carefully before buying one!

Don't forget

Apple's website (http://www.apple.com/support/ipad/using/) has lots of helpful tips on using the iPad.

NEW

The New icon pictured above indicates a new or enhanced feature introduced on the iPad with the latest version of the operating system: iOS 12.

iPad Specifications

Since its introduction there are now several different generations of iPad, including the iPad mini, which is smaller than both the original iPad and the larger iPad Pro. When considering which iPad is best for you, some of the specifications to consider are:

- **Processor**: This determines the speed at which the iPad operates and how quickly tasks are performed.

- **Storage**: This determines how much content you can store on your iPad. Across the latest models in the iPad family, the range of storage is from 32GB to 1TB.

- **Connectivity**: The options for this are Wi-Fi and 3G/4G connectivity for the internet, and Bluetooth for connecting to other devices over short distances. All models of iPad have Wi-Fi connectivity as standard.

- **Screen**: Look for an iPad with a Retina Display screen for the highest resolution and best clarity. This is an LED-backlit screen and is available on the iPad Pro, the iPad Air 2 (and later) and the iPad mini 3 (and later).

- **Operating System**: The iPad Pro, the iPad and the iPad mini all run on the iOS 12 operating system.

- **Battery Power**: This is the length of time the iPad can be used for general use such as surfing the web on Wi-Fi, watching video, or listening to music. All models offer approximately 10 hours of use in this way.

- **Input/Output**: The iPad Pro, the iPad and the iPad mini have similar output/input options. These are a Lightning Connector port (for charging), 3.5 mm stereo headphone minijack, built-in speaker, microphone, and micro-SIM card tray (Wi-Fi and 4G model only).

- **Sensors**: These are used to access the amount of ambient light and also the orientation in which the iPad is being held. The sensors include an accelerometer, ambient light sensor, and gyroscope.

- **TV and Video**: This determines how your iPad can be connected to a High Definition TV. This is done with AirPlay Mirroring, which lets you send what's on your iPad screen to an HDTV wirelessly with AppleTV.

Beware

If you have a fourth-generation iPad (or later) then it'll come with the Lightning Connector. You'll need to buy adapters to connect it to your "old" 30-pin accessories such as TV, iPod dock, etc.

Lightning Connector Adapter

30-pin Dock Connector

Lightning Connector

Models and Sizes

Since its introduction in 2010, the iPad has evolved in both its size and specifications. It is now a family of devices, rather than a single-size tablet. When choosing your iPad, the first consideration is which size to select. There are three options:

iOS 12, the latest version of the operating system used by iPads, can be used on all iPads that were capable of running iOS 11. iOS 12 contains a range of performance improvements; the new Screen Time feature for monitoring the amount of time spent on your iPad; Siri Shortcuts for creating a sequence of actions with one trigger word; the new Measure app for measuring items; and updated versions of Apple Books and Photos. To check the version of the iOS, look in **Settings** > **General** > **Software Update**.

- **Standard iPad**. This is the original size of the iPad. It measures 9.7 inches (diagonally) and has a high-resolution Retina Display screen. Some versions have been called iPad Air, and the latest version, at the time of printing, is the sixth generation of the standard-size iPad, which also supports the Apple Pencil.

- **iPad mini**. The iPad mini is similar in most respects to the larger version, including the Retina Display screen, except for its size. The screen is 7.9 inches (diagonally) and it is also slightly lighter. The latest version, at the time of printing, is the iPad mini 4.

- **iPad Pro**. This is the latest size of the iPad to be introduced (first announced in September 2015), and is aimed more as a replacement for laptop computers. The latest versions come without a Home button (see next page for details). The iPad Pro can also be used with the Apple Pencil stylus, the detachable Apple Smart Keyboard, and the Smart Keyboard Folio (all bought separately).

In terms of functionality there is little difference between the standard iPad and the iPad mini, and the choice may depend on the size of screen that you prefer. The iPad Air 2 (and later, standard iPad), the iPad mini 3 (and later) and the iPad Pro (except the latest models; see next page) have Touch ID functionality, whereby the Home button can be used as a fingerprint sensor for unlocking the iPad.

Another variation in the iPad family is how they connect to the internet and online services. There are two options:

- **With Wi-Fi connectivity**. This enables you to connect to the internet via a Wi-Fi router, either in your own home or at a Wi-Fi hotspot.

- **With Wi-Fi and 4G connectivity (where available, but it also covers 3G)**. This should be considered if you will need to connect to the internet with a cellular connection.

No Home Button iPad Pro

In October 2018 Apple announced the latest range of iPad Pro models: a 12.9-inch version and an 11-inch version. Both models have a high-quality Liquid Retina screen that virtually goes to the edge of the iPads. The most significant difference between the latest iPad Pros and previous versions is that they do not have a Home button, which is the first time this has been the case on the iPad. Because of this, the functions that were previously done with the Home button are now done using a selection of swipes and actions:

- **Unlocking the iPad**. This is done by using Face ID. Once this has been set up (see New tip), raise the iPad so that the camera can view your face, and simultaneously swipe up from the bottom of the screen. This can be done in portrait and landscape screen orientation.

- **Returning to the Home screen**. Swipe up from the bar at the bottom of the screen. This can be done from any app.

- **Accessing the Dock**. Perform a short swipe up from the bar at the bottom of the screen and stop when the Dock appears.

- **Accessing the App Switcher.** Swipe up from the bottom of the screen and pause in the middle of the screen to view open and recently-used apps.

- **Accessing Siri**. Press and hold the On/Off button until Siri appears. Alternatively, use the Hey Siri function (see page 23).

At the time of printing, the 12.9-inch and 11-inch iPad Pros are the only iPad models that do not have a Home button. Therefore, throughout the book the functionality that is detailed will refer to the range of iPads that do have a Home button.

Using Face ID is a new feature on the iPad Pro. It can be set up in **Settings** > **Face ID and Passcode** > **Set Up Face ID.** Position your face in the circle and the camera will map your face for Face ID. The process will be done twice, and when it is completed you will be able to unlock your iPad by swiping up from the bottom of the screen (landscape or portrait) and looking at the camera. The camera uses a TrueDepth system to accurately map faces.

Finding Your Way Around

The physical buttons and controls on the iPad are very simple. Additional functions such as screen brightness are software-controlled, in the Settings app or the Control Center.

When you first unpack your iPad you will also find a Lightning/USB cable for charging the iPad or connecting it to a computer. There will also be a USB power adapter for charging the iPad. There is a range of iPad accessories available from the Apple Store, one of the most useful being a Smart Cover for protecting the iPad and also putting it to sleep when not in use.

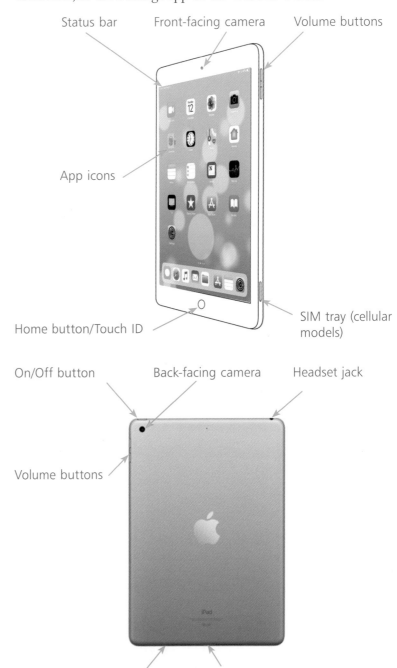

Status bar

Front-facing camera

Volume buttons

App icons

Home button/Touch ID

SIM tray (cellular models)

On/Off button

Back-facing camera

Headset jack

Volume buttons

Speakers

Lightning Connector

The **network data icons** at the top of the screen are those that mostly relate to the communications connections in the Settings app; e.g. Wi-Fi, Bluetooth and Cellular.

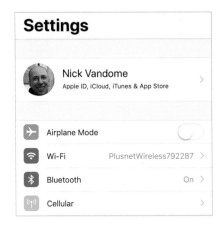

The fastest data connection is Wi-Fi. If no Wi-Fi is available you will need to use 3G/4G (if your iPad has this option), which is fairly fast. Unfortunately, as you move around, the 3G/4G signal will come and go so you may see the 3G/4G disappear and be replaced by the EDGE symbol (E). EDGE is slower than 3G/4G.

If you're *really* unlucky, the EDGE signal may vanish and you may see the GPRS symbol. GPRS is *very* slow!

o	GPRS (slowest)	✈	Location services
E	EDGE	🔒	Lock
3G	3G	LTE	LTE
4G	4G	⌾	Personal Hotspot
📶	Wi-Fi	▶	Play
✳	Bluetooth	@	Screen lock
✈	Airplane mode	↻	Syncing
⁂	iPad is busy		

The GPRS, EDGE and 3G/4G icons are seen on the models featuring both Wi-Fi and cellular only.

Don't forget

The iPad has many features that make it accessible to those with specific visual and audio needs. These features are covered in detail on pages 230-234.

Home Button

There are very few actual physical buttons on the iPad, but the Home button is an important one. The Home button performs a number of functions, including accessing the App Switcher window where you can view your active apps and close them if required.

Home button functions:

You can see your active apps by bringing up the App Switcher window. If an app is misbehaving, quit it using the App Switcher window (see page 19).

- If you are on any other screen other than the original Home screen (i.e. the one that appears when you first turn on your iPad), press the Home button to go back to the Home screen: this saves you having to flick the screens to the left.

- Pressing the Home button quickly twice brings up the App Switcher window (shows your active apps).

To see the App Switcher window without having to press the Home button twice, drag four fingers up the screen. You can also drag four fingers right or left across the screen to switch between open apps.

- From any screen, press and hold the Home button to access Siri, the iPad's digital voice assistant.

Note: The latest models of the iPad Pro (announced October 2018) do not have a Home button. The functions performed by the Home button are replaced by a range of gestures and button presses (see page 13 for details).

For more on swiping, tapping and pinching for getting around, see page 27.

16

The Home screen is the first screen you see when you start up the iPad. It contains the apps installed by Apple, which cannot be deleted. In all, there are 29 of these – five will be on the Dock.

The Dock comes with five apps attached. You can move these off, add other apps, or you can put your favorite apps there and remove those placed on the Dock by Apple. The Dock has a dividing line, and recently-used apps appear to the right of it.

You can move these apps to other screens if you want to, but it's a good idea to keep the most important or most frequently-used apps on this screen.

The Stocks and Voice Memo apps are now pre-installed on the iPad; in some previous versions of iOS they had to be downloaded separately, from the App Store. The Measure app is a new app.

By default, there are five apps to the left of the dividing line on the Dock at the bottom of the screen. You can add more if needed, up to a total of 13. You can even drag folders to the Dock. To add items to the Dock, press and hold on them and drag them onto the Dock when they start to jiggle.

17

Time and Date   Network connections   Battery

Wallpaper

Pre-installed apps

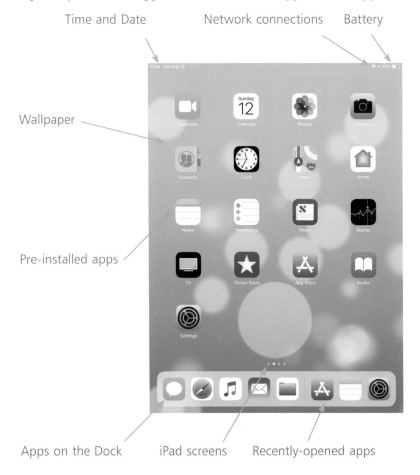

To move an app, press and hold on it until it starts to jiggle. Then, drag it into a new position or onto the Dock. To move an app to another screen, press and hold on it and move it to the edge of the screen, until the next screen appears.

Apps on the Dock   iPad screens   Recently-opened apps

App Switcher Window

Since the iPad can run several apps at once, it is useful to be able to view all of the apps that are open, and close them if required. This management feature is done with the App Switcher window and it can perform a number of tasks:

● It shows open apps.

● It enables you to move between open apps and open different ones.

● It enables apps to be closed (see next page).

Accessing App Switcher

The App Switcher window can be accessed from any screen on your iPad, as follows:

Don't forget

On the models of iPad Pro with no Home button, the App Switcher is accessed by swiping up from the bar at the bottom of the screen, and pausing in the middle of the screen, when the App Switcher should appear.

1 Double-click on the **Home** button (or swipe up the screen with four fingers)

2 The currently-open apps are displayed, with their icons above them (except the Home screen). The most recently-used apps are shown at the right-hand side

3 Swipe left and right to view the open apps. Tap on one to access it in full-screen size

Closing Items

The iPad deals with open apps very efficiently. They do not interact with other apps, which increases security and also means that they can be left open in the background, without using up a significant amount of processing power, in a state of semi-hibernation until they are needed. Because of this, it is not essential to close apps when you move to something else. However, you may want to close apps if you feel you have too many open or if one stops working. To do this:

1 Access the App Switcher window. The currently-open apps are displayed

2 Press and hold on an app and swipe it to the top of the screen to close it. This does not remove it from the iPad and it can be opened again in the usual way

3 The app is removed from its position in the App Switcher window

Don't forget

When you switch from one app to another, the first one stays open in the background. You can go back to it by accessing it from the App Switcher window or the Home screen.

In the Control Center

The Control Center is a panel containing some of the most commonly-used options within the **Settings** app. It can be accessed with one swipe and is an excellent function for when you do not want to go into Settings.

Accessing the Control Center

The Control Center can be accessed from any screen within iOS 12, and it can also be accessed from the Lock Screen. To enable the Control Center to be accessed from all apps:

1 Tap on the **Settings** app

The Control Center cannot be disabled from being accessed from the Home screen.

2 Tap on the **Control Center** option and drag the

Access Within Apps buttons On or Off, to specify if the Control Center can be accessed from all apps

3 Swipe down from the top right-hand corner of any screen to access the Control Center panel

The method for accessing the Control Center is a new feature on the iPad with iOS 12.

...cont'd

Control Center controls

The items that can be used in the Control Center include:

1 Use these controls for any music or video that is playing. Use the buttons to Pause/Play a track, go to the beginning or end, and drag the slider to adjust the volume

2 Tap on this button to turn **Airplane mode** On or Off

3 Tap on this button to turn **Wi-Fi** On or Off

4 Tap on this button to turn **Bluetooth** On or Off

5 Tap on this button to turn **Do Not Disturb** mode On or Off

6 Tap on this button to access a clock, including a stopwatch

7 Tap on this button to open the **Camera** app

8 Drag here to adjust the screen brightness

9 Tap on this button to **Lock** or **Unlock** screen rotation. If it is locked, the screen will not change when you change the orientation of your iPad

Hot tip

The items that appear in the Control Center can be customized: select **Settings** > **Control Center** > **Customize Controls**. Tap on a red icon next to an item to remove it from the Control Center; tap on a green icon next to an item to add it to the Control Center.

Don't forget

Another Control Center option is Screen Mirroring, which can be used to display the content of your iPad on your TV. You'll need Apple TV connected to the TV. (Apple TV is sold separately.)

21

Finding Things on the iPad

Sometimes you haven't got time to look through your entire calendar for an appointment, or to scroll through iTunes for one track. You can use Spotlight (Apple's indexing and search facility) to find specific apps, contacts, emails, appointments, and music content.

Start search

Hot tip

Search using Spotlight to avoid spending ages looking for emails, music tracks and other data.

1 From any free area on the Home screen, press and hold and swipe downwards

2 You will be taken to the Spotlight Search screen

Don't forget

Spotlight can search over a range of areas, including nearby restaurants, movies, and locations.

3 Enter your search word or phrase into the Search box

4 Your results will show up below. The results are grouped according to their type; i.e. Calendar appointment, email, etc.

Finding Things with Siri

Siri is the iPad's digital voice assistant that provides answers to a variety of questions by looking on your iPad and also at web services. You can ask Siri questions relating to the apps on your iPad, and also general questions such as weather conditions around the world, or sports results. To set up Siri:

1. Open **Settings** > **General**, then tap on the **Siri** link

2. Drag the **Siri** button to **On** to activate the Siri functionality

Questioning Siri

Once you have set up Siri, you can start putting it to work with your queries. To do this:

1. Hold down the **Home** button until the Siri window appears

2. If you do not ask anything initially, Siri will prompt you with some suggestions (or tap on the **?** button in the bottom left-hand corner for more suggestions)

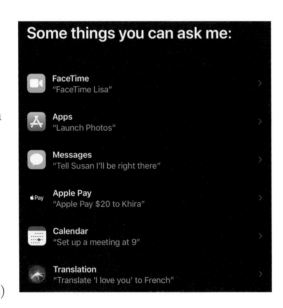

Some things you can ask me:

FaceTime
"FaceTime Lisa"

Apps
"Launch Photos"

Messages
"Tell Susan I'll be right there"

Apple Pay
"Apple Pay $20 to Khira"

Calendar
"Set up a meeting at 9"

Translation
"Translate 'I love you' to French"

3. Tap on this button to ask a question of Siri

On the models of iPad Pro with no Home button, Siri can be accessed by holding down the On/Off button.

Turn **On** the **Allow "Hey Siri"** button in the Siri Settings to activate Siri just by saying this, without having to press the Home button (when connected to power).

Within the Siri Settings you can select a language and a voice style.

Multitasking on the iPad

The iPad has evolved from being an internet-enabled communication and entertainment device into something that is now a genuine productivity device. With iOS 12, productivity options enable the iPad to display more than one app at a time on the screen (only with certain models of iPad). This means that it can be easier to get tasks done, as you can see content from two apps at once.

Slide Over

Slide Over is an option that is available on the iPad, iPad Pro, iPad mini 2 (and later) and iPad Air (and later). It enables you to activate a second app as a floating bar while another app is open at full screen below it. To do this:

1 Open the first app that you want to use

2 Swipe up from the bottom of the screen to access the Dock

3 Press and hold on an app on the Dock and drag it over the first app

4 Release the second app. Regardless of where it is positioned, it will snap to the right-hand side of the screen as a floating bar over the first app

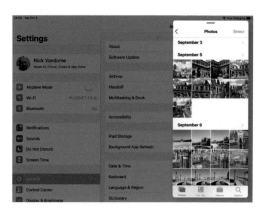

Hot tip

The **Picture in Picture** function enables a FaceTime or YouTube video to be minimized on the screen but remain active so that you can still view and perform other tasks at the same time.

Split View

On the iPad Pro and iPad Air 2 (and later), the concept of Slide Over is taken one step further by Split View: the second item can become a fixed item, which can then be resized so that it has equal prominence to the first app. To do this:

1 Open the first app that you want to use

2 Swipe up from the bottom of the screen to access the Dock

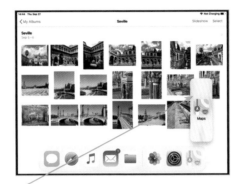

Swipe the button on the middle bar left or right to make either panel full-screen.

3 Press and hold on an app on the Dock and drag it to the right-hand or left-hand side of the screen, and release the app when a dark bar appears below it

4 Initially, the app in Split View takes up 30% of the screen and can be used independently of the other app

5 Drag on the middle button to change the proportions of the two Split View panels

Default Applications

These are some of the most popular pre-installed apps:

Don't forget

The rest of the pre-installed apps are: the **Stocks** app, for viewing financial information; the **Tips** app, for viewing tips about using iOS 12; the **Podcasts** app, for downloading and listening to audio podcasts; the **Find iPhone** app, for finding a lost Apple device; the **Find Friends** app, for locating an Apple device belonging to family or friends; the **Voice Memos** app, for recording voice messages; and the **Measure** app, for measuring items.

NEW

The FaceTime app can be used to make video and voice calls to other FaceTime users. This can be done with up to 32 other people. This is known as Group FaceTime and is a new feature in iOS 12. See page 90 for details.

Calendar: keeps your appointments in sync with your other Apple devices, using iCloud.

Contacts: lists all contacts including phone numbers, email, postal addresses and notes.

Notes: for jotting things down. Store notes within iCloud so that they are available on other devices.

Maps: GPS-enabled maps help you get from A to B, and show current position and other information.

TV: play movies and other video content, purchased or from your own collection.

iTunes Store: browse and buy music, movies, TV shows and more.

App Store: your central store for paid and free apps.

Reminders: to-do lists, sync with Apple Mail and Outlook Tasks.

Messages: send SMS-type messages free with Wi-Fi to other compatible devices.

Settings: this is where you make changes to personalize your iPad.

Safari: Apple's home-grown web browser.

Mail: handles IMAP and POP3 email, and syncs to your main accounts on your computer.

Photos: show your photos with slideshows, print off photos or share via Facebook, Twitter, etc.

Music: controls music and provides access to the Apple Music subscription service.

Books: this can be used to download and read ebooks.

Camera: shoot stills or movies using front or back cameras, similar to iPhone functionality.

FaceTime: video chat to others using iPad, iPhone or Mac.

Photo Booth: take still images and select from a series of special effects.

News: collates news content from numerous sources (not yet available in all locations).

Clock: provides time in any part of the world. Useful as an alarm clock and a stopwatch.

The Display and Keyboard

So, what's so exciting about the screen? What makes it so special? Firstly, it has a high-quality Retina Display.

The technology behind the multitouch screen is ingenious. Using one, two, three or four fingers you can do lots of different things on the iPad, depending on the app you're using and what you want to do. The main actions are tap, flick, pinch/spread, and drag.

The screen is designed to be used with fingers – the skin on glass contact is required (if you tap using your nail you will find it won't work). There are also styluses that can be used with the iPad, including the Apple Pencil for the standard iPad and iPad Pro.

Tap	Apps open when you tap their icons. Within apps you can select photos, music, web links and many other functions. The tap is similar to a single click with a mouse on the computer.
Flick	You can flick through lists like Contacts, Songs, or anywhere there's a long list. Place your finger on the screen and quickly flick up and down and the list scrolls rapidly up and down.
Pinch/spread	The iPad screen responds to two fingers placed on its surface. To reduce the size of a photo or web page in Safari place two fingers on the screen and bring them together. To enlarge the image or web page spread your fingers apart and the image grows in size.
Drag	You can drag web pages and maps around if you are unable to see the edges. Simply place your finger on the screen and keep it there but move the image or web page around until you can see the hidden areas.

Hot tip

Use four fingers to bring up the App Switcher window (drag four fingers up the screen), or flick right or left using four fingers to switch between running apps.

...cont'd

The iPad is different to a laptop since there is no physical keyboard. Instead, you type by tapping the **virtual keyboard** on the iPad screen itself. You can use the keyboard in portrait or landscape modes. The landscape version provides much wider keys.

The keyboard seems to change in different apps

The keyboard is smart – and should match the app you're in. For example, if you are word processing or entering regular text you will see a standard keyboard. But if you are using a browser or are prompted to enter an email address, you will see a modified keyboard with *.com* and @ symbols prominently displayed.

The iPad Pro is designed to work with the Apple Smart Keyboard and the Smart Keyboard Folio (sold separately).

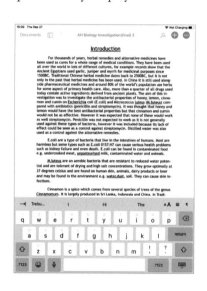

If you have Wi-Fi, try using your voice to dictate emails and other text using the Dictate option (its icon is on the left of the spacebar).

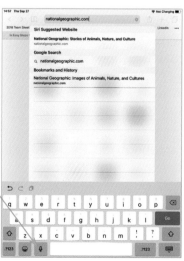

Top left: portrait keyboard in Mail.

Top right: portrait keyboard in Pages.

Bottom left: portrait keyboard in Safari – note the **Return** key has now changed to **Go**. Tap this to search the web or go to a specific URL.

Hot tip

If you find you are making lots of typing errors, try switching the iPad to landscape mode (keys are larger).

Mail with iPad in the landscape position. Notice how wide the keys have become, making it easier to type without hitting two keys at once! Also notice the Dictation icon to the left of the spacebar (you get this when connected to Wi-Fi).

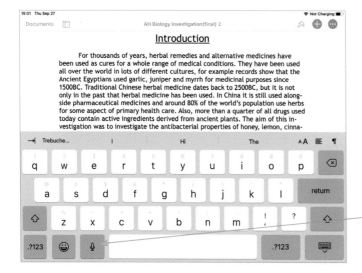

Don't forget

To ensure dictation is activated (denoted by the microphone icon to the left of the spacebar), select **Settings** > **General** > **Keyboard** and turn the **Enable Dictation** button to **On**.

Pages with landscape keyboard. Again, the keyboard is large, but the downside is that you lose real estate for work – the effective area for viewing content is quite small.

Caps Lock and Auto-Correct

It's annoying when you want to type something entirely in uppercase letters, since you have to press Shift for every letter – or do you? Actually, there's a setting that will activate Caps Lock but you need to activate this in Settings:

1. Go to **Settings**

2. Select **General**

3. Select **Keyboard**

4. Make sure the **Enable Caps Lock** slider is set to **On**

5. While you are there, make sure the other settings are On; for example, the **"." Shortcut** (see below)

Hot tip

If you do not like the default iPad keyboard, you can download other third-party virtual ones from the App Store. Two to look at are: SwiftKey, and KuaiBoard.

Other settings for the keyboard

- **Auto-Correction** suggests the correct word. If it annoys you, switch it off.

- **Auto-Capitalization** is great for putting capitals in names.

- The **"." Shortcut** types a period/full stop every time you hit the spacebar twice. This saves time when typing long emails but if you prefer not to use this, switch it off. Here's another neat trick – you can also insert a period/full stop by tapping the spacebar with two fingers simultaneously.

As you type words, the iPad **Auto-Correct** will suggest words intelligently, which will speed up your typing.

To accept iPad suggestion

When the suggested word pops up, simply tap the spacebar and it will be inserted. The suggested word may not be what you want, in which case you can reject it by tapping the "x" next to the suggested word.

To reject suggestion

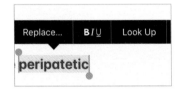

Above left: The iPad will suggest a word but if you don't want to use the suggestion tap the "x" next to it. The word you type will be added to your user dictionary.

Above right: You can look up the dictionary: tap the word twice, tap the right arrow and choose **Look Up**.

Using an External Keyboard

There are times when you need real physical keys; for example, if you are typing a longer document you might find tapping out your text on the glass screen annoying. There are three main options for this:

- A wired external keyboard that connects via the iPad's Lightning Connector.

- A third-party Bluetooth keyboard, which can be connected wirelessly via the iPad's internal Bluetooth.

- The Apple Smart Keyboard and Smart Keyboard Folio. This is used with the iPad Pro and attaches via the Smart Connector on the keyboard and the iPad.

Keyboard Tricks

Although it's not immediately obvious, the keyboard can generate accents, acutes, and many other foreign characters and symbols.

Holding the letters "a", "e", "i", "o" or "u" generates lots of variants. Just slide your finger along till you reach the one you want and it will be inserted into the document.

Hot tip

For accents and other additional characters, touch the key then slide your finger to the character you want to use.

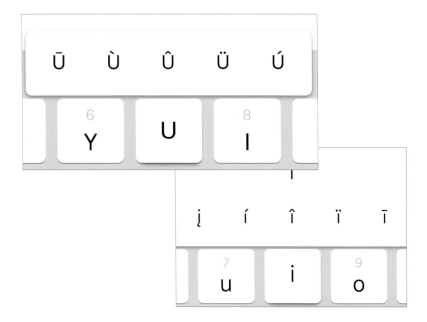

Also, when you use Safari you don't have to enter ".com", ".org", etc. in URLs – the **?** key will produce other endings if you touch and hold the key.

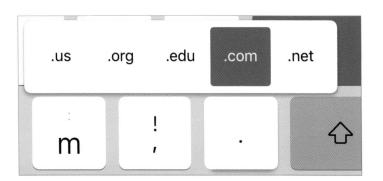

Select, Copy and Paste Text

Rather than retype text, you can select text (or pictures) and paste these into other documents or the URL field in Safari. Touch and hold text, images or URLs (links) to open, save or copy them.

To select text

Touch and hold a paragraph of text to select. Drag the handles to enclose the text you want to copy then tap **Copy**.

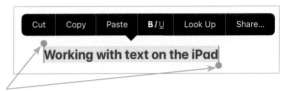

Copy web links by tapping and selecting **Copy**. If you just want to go to the website, click **Open in New Tab**.

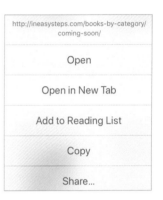

Use the built-in dictionary by tapping a word then **Look Up**.

Paste copied text or images by tapping the screen in Pages, for example, and tapping on the **Paste** button.

Editing Text

Once text has been entered it can be selected, copied, cut and pasted. Depending on the app being used, the text can also be formatted, such as with a word processing app.

Selecting text
To select text and perform tasks on it:

1 To change the insertion point, tap and hold until the magnifying glass appears

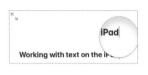

2 Drag the magnifying glass to move the insertion point

3 Tap at the insertion point to access the menu buttons

4 Double-tap on a word to select it. Tap on one of the menu buttons as required

5 Drag the selection handles to expand or contract the selection

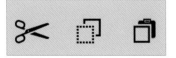

6 Use the Shortcuts bar on the keyboard to, from left to right, cut the selection, copy the selection, or paste the selection

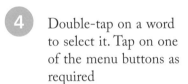

Hot tip

Once the menu buttons have been accessed, tap on **Select** to select the previous word, or **Select All** to select all of the text.

Hot tip

The menu buttons in Step 4 can also be used to replace the selected word, add bold, italics or underlining to it, or look up a definition of it.

Hot tip

In some apps, the cursor can be moved by dragging anywhere on the screen with two fingers, including over the keyboard. Text can then be selected by single- or double-tapping.

Using Predictive Text

Predictive text tries to guess what you are typing, and also predicts the next word following the one you have just typed. It was developed primarily for text messaging and it can be used on the iPad with iOS 12. To do this:

1 Tap on the **General** tab in the Settings app

2 Tap on the **Keyboard** option

3 Drag the **Predictive** button **On**

4 When predictive text is activated, the QuickType bar is displayed above the keyboard. Initially, this has a suggestion for the first word to include. Tap on a word or start typing

5 As you type, suggestions appear. Tap on one to accept it. Tap on the word within the quotation marks to accept exactly what you have typed

6 After you have typed a word, a suggestion for the next word appears.
Tap on it to use it, or ignore it if you wish

Don't forget

Predictive text learns from your writing style as you write, and so gets more accurate at predicting words. It can also recognize a change in style for different apps, such as Mail and Messages.

2 Getting Started

As with most technology, although the iPad is plug-and-play, there is some initial setting up to do. It's worth spending some time setting up the iPad so it best suits your needs for work and play.

Turn On and Off

You can put your iPad fully Off, or into sleep mode (sleep mode is useful because as soon as you press the Home button the iPad is instantly On).

- If the iPad is fully Off, press and hold the **On/Off** button – the iPad will start up.

- When you have finished using it, simply press the **On/Off** button briefly and the iPad will enter sleep mode.

- Sleep mode uses very little power so for the sake of speed, simply use sleep mode unless you are not going to use the iPad for several days.

- To wake from sleep, press the **Home** button or **On/Off** button.

- The Lock Screen will be displayed. Swipe the **Press home to open** option to the right to access the Home screen.

Use sleep mode to turn your iPad off unless you are not planning to use it for an extended period.

On the models of iPad Pro with no Home button, the iPad can be woken from sleep by swiping up from the bottom of the screen and looking at the camera to use Face ID for waking and unlocking the iPad.

To fully power off

1 Press and hold the **On/Off** button until you see the slider bar and **slide to power off** appears

2 Slide this button to the right

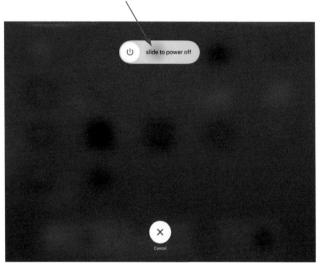

3 The iPad will fully shut down

Lock the screen

The iPad works in portrait (upright) and landscape (sideways) modes. The iPad is clever and can tell which way up it is being held and the screen will rotate accordingly. Sometimes you will want it to stay fixed in portrait or landscape modes. This can be done with the Screen Lock function. This can be controlled using the Control Center. To do this, swipe down from the top right-hand corner of the screen and tap on this button.

Syncing with iTunes

The iPad and iOS 12 are both very much linked to the online world, and the iCloud service can be used to store and synchronize several types of content. However, it is still possible to use iTunes on a Mac or PC to sync content, including: music, videos, apps, TV shows, podcasts and books. To do this:

Beware

When you are syncing items to your iPad it is best to select specific folders or files, rather than including everything. This is because items such as music, videos and photos can take up a lot of storage space on your iPad if you sync a large library from your computer.

Hot tip

On the **Summary** page accessed from Step 1, scroll down to view the options for syncing, such as specifying only checked songs and videos to be synced, or manually manage music and videos for syncing.

40

1 Connect your iPad to your computer. iTunes should open automatically but if it does not, launch it in the usual way. Click on this button to access the iPad and click on the **Summary** tab to view general details about your iPad

2 iTunes can be used to back up your iPad to the attached computer (in addition to iCloud). To do this, click on the **This Computer** button under the **Backups** section and click on the **Back Up Now** button

3 Click on the categories in the panel in Step 1 to select the items that you want to sync. These include Music, Films (Movies), TV Programmes (TV Shows), Podcasts, Books, Photos, and details from apps and files. Select what you want to sync for each heading (this can be for all items in a category or selected items)

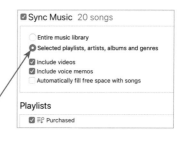

4 Click on the **Done** button to start the sync process and copy the selected items to your iPad

Using iCloud

iCloud is a service that allows you to use the Cloud to sync your data (including Calendars, Contacts, Mail, Safari bookmarks, and Notes) wirelessly.

Once you are registered and set up, any entries or deletions to Calendars and other apps are reflected in all devices using iCloud.

An Apple ID is required for using iCloud, and this can be obtained online at **https://appleid.apple.com/** or you can create an Apple ID when you first access an app on your iPad that requires this for use. It is free to create an Apple ID, and requires a username and password. Once you have created an Apple ID you can then use the full range of iCloud services.

iCloud settings

Once you have set up your iCloud account you can then apply settings for how it works. Once you have done this, you will not have to worry about it again:

The iPad apps that require an Apple ID to access their full functionality include: iTunes Store, Messages, Books, FaceTime, and the App Store.

1 Access the **iCloud** section in the Settings app

2 Tap on the **iCloud** button

3 Drag these buttons to **On** for each item that you wish to be synced with iCloud. Each item is then saved and stored in the iCloud and made available to your other iCloud-enabled devices

...cont'd

Using iCloud online

Once you have created an Apple ID you will automatically have an iCloud account. This can be used to sync your data from your iPad, and you can also access your content online from the iCloud website at **www.icloud.com**

1 Enter your Apple ID details

2 The full range of iCloud apps is displayed, including those for Pages, Numbers, and Keynote

3 Click on an app to view its details. If iCloud is set up on your iPad, any changes made here will be displayed in the online app too

Find my iPad

This is a great feature that allows you to see where your devices are. Once activated (**Settings** > **Apple ID** > **iCloud** > **Find My iPad**), sign in to iCloud using a web browser on any computer and click **Find My iPhone**. This will find your iPad and any other devices you have registered.

When you register for iCloud you automatically create an iCloud email account, which can be used on your iPad and also online.

42

iCloud provides 5GB free storage but you can pay for more (*correct at the time of printing*).

About the iCloud Drive

One of the options in the iCloud section is for the iCloud Drive. This can be used to store documents so that you can use them on any other Apple devices that you have, such as an iPhone or a MacBook. With iCloud Drive (and the Files app) you can start work on a document on one device and continue on another device from where you left off.

1 Tap on the **Apple ID** tab of the Settings app

2 Tap on the **iCloud** button

3 By default, the iCloud Drive is set to **Off**

4 Slide the **iCloud Drive** button to green to turn it **On**

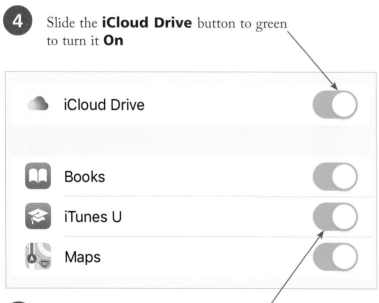

5 Drag the buttons **On** for the apps that you want to activate for syncing files with iCloud Drive. Content that you create with these apps will be stored in the iCloud Drive and be available within the same apps on other devices

Don't forget

Some third-party apps are compatible with the iCloud Drive, but the standard ones are some of Apple's own apps such as Pages, Numbers and Keynote.

43

Beware

To access documents on iCloud Drive on other devices, these devices need to have iCloud Drive turned **On** and activated for the required apps.

Using the Files App

Once the iCloud Drive has been activated within the iCloud settings, documents can be viewed and accessed using the Files app. This can be used to store documents and files that have been created on the iPad and also other online storage services, such as Dropbox and Google Drive. To start using the Files app:

1 Tap on the **Files** app

By default, the Files app is on the Dock.

2 The Files app window shows items that are stored there, as specified by the selection in Step 5 on page 43

3 Tap on the **iCloud Drive** button and tap on a folder to view its contents. By default, the documents are stored in the iCloud. Tap on an item to open it and download it to your iPad

Tap on this button on the top toolbar to add a new folder to the top level of the Files app, or within any of the existing folders.

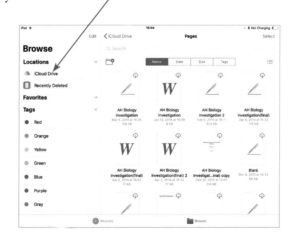

4 Tap on the **Select** button on the top toolbar

Select

5 Tap on items to select them

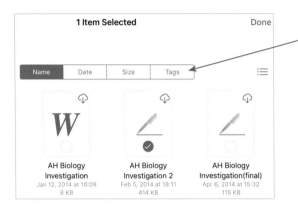

1 Item Selected   Done

| Name | Date | Size | Tags |

AH Biology
Investigation
Jan 12, 2014 at 18:09
8 KB

AH Biology
Investigation 2
Feb 5, 2014 at 18:11
414 KB

AH Biology
Investigation(final)
Apr 6, 2014 at 15:32
115 KB

Hot tip

Tap on these buttons to view items in a folder according to, from left to right, **Name**, **Date** modified, **Size** and **Tags** that have been added (see tip below).

| Name | Date | Size | Tags |

6 Use the buttons on the bottom toolbar to **Duplicate**, **Move**, **Share** or **Delete** the selected item(s)

| Duplicate | Move | Share | Delete |

Hot tip

Drag a file over one of the tags in the left-hand panel to add the tag to the document, to help identify it.

7 If you have an account with online Cloud-sharing services such as Dropbox or Google Drive, these will be available via the Files app, once you have downloaded the apps from the App Store and logged into them

Edit

Browse

Locations   ⌄

⚄ Dropbox

☁ iCloud Drive

Don't forget

Tap on a location other than iCloud Drive (i.e. Dropbox) to view its folder structure. Tap on items within the folders to download them to your iPad.

8 Tap on the **Edit** button in the previous step to show or hide the items by dragging their buttons **On** or **Off**

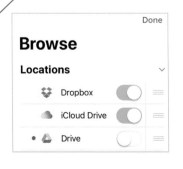

Done

Browse

Locations   ⌄

⚄ Dropbox   🔵

☁ iCloud Drive 🔵

• ▲ Drive   ⚪

About Family Sharing

As everyone gets more and more digital devices, it is becoming increasingly important to be able to share content with other people, particularly family members. In iOS 12, the Family Sharing function enables you to share items that you have downloaded from the App Store, such as music and movies, with up to six other family members, as long as they have an Apple ID account. Once this has been set up, it is also possible to share items such as family calendars and photos, and even see where family members are, on a map. To set up and start using Family Sharing:

1 Access the **iCloud** section within the Settings app, as shown on page 43

2 Tap on the **Set Up Family Sharing...** link

Set Up Family Sharing...

3 Tap on the **Get Started** button

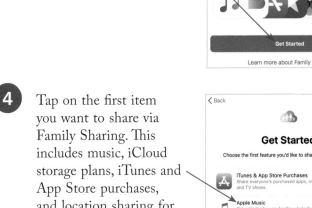

Family Sharing

Share music, movies, apps, storage and more with up to six members of your family.

You'll also get a family photo album, family calendar, and access to family devices in Find My iPhone.

Get Started

Learn more about Family Sharing

4 Tap on the first item you want to share via Family Sharing. This includes music, iCloud storage plans, iTunes and App Store purchases, and location sharing for finding a lost or stolen Apple device

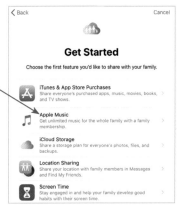

‹ Back   Cancel

Get Started

Choose the first feature you'd like to share with your family.

iTunes & App Store Purchases
Share everyone's purchased apps, music, movies, books, and TV shows.

Apple Music
Get unlimited music for the whole family with a family membership.

iCloud Storage
Share a storage plan for everyone's photos, files, and backups.

Location Sharing
Share your location with family members in Messages and Find My Friends.

Screen Time
Stay engaged in and help your family develop good habits with their screen time.

Don't forget

To use Family Sharing, other family members must have an Apple device using either iOS 8 (or later) for a mobile device (iPad, iPhone or iPod Touch) or OS X Yosemite (or later) for a desktop or laptop Mac computer.

...cont'd

5 Tap on the **Continue** button again to confirm your Apple ID account for Family Sharing

6 If you are the organizer of Family Sharing, payments will be taken from the credit/debit card that you registered when you set up your Apple ID. Tap on the **Continue** button to confirm this

7 Once Family Sharing has been created, return to the iCloud section in the Settings app and tap on the **Invite Family Members** button

Hot tip

If children are added to Family Sharing you can specify that they have to ask permission before downloading content from the iTunes Store, the App Store or the Book Store. To do this, select them in the **Family Sharing** section of the **iCloud** settings and drag the **Ask To Buy** button to **On**. Each time they want to buy something you will be sent a notification asking for approval.

47

8 Enter the name or email address of a family member, and tap on the **Send** button

9 An invitation is sent to the selected person. They have to accept this before they can participate in Family Sharing

Using Family Sharing

Once you have set up Family Sharing and added family members, you can start sharing a selection of items.

Sharing photos

Photos can be shared with Family Sharing thanks to the Family album that is created automatically within the Photos app. To use this:

Beware

iCloud Photo sharing has to be turned **On** to enable Family Sharing (**Settings** > **Photos** > **iCloud Photos**).

1 Tap on the **Photos** app

2 Tap on the **Albums** button

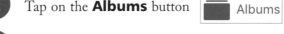

3 The **Family** album is already available in the **Shared Albums** section

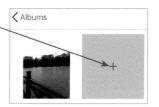

4 Tap on this button to add photos to the album

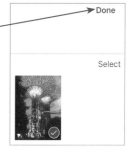

Hot tip

When someone else in your Family Sharing circle adds a photo to the Family album, you are notified in the Notification Center and also by a red notification on the Photos app.

5 Tap on the photos you want to add, and tap on the **Done** button

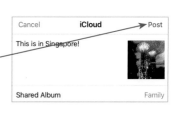

6 Make sure the **Family** album is selected as the Shared Album, and tap on the **Post** button

Sharing calendars

Family Sharing also generates a Family calendar that can be used by all Family Sharing members:

1   Tap on the **Calendar** app

2   Create a calendar event, as shown on pages 116-117, tap on the **Calendar** button and select the **Family** calendar to add the event to a calendar that all members of Family Sharing can see

Hot tip

To change the color tag for a calendar, tap on the Calendar button at the bottom-middle of the Calendar window. All of the current calendars will be shown. Tap on the **i** symbol next to a calendar, and select a new color as required.

Sharing music, books and movies

Family Sharing means that all members of the group can share purchases from the iTunes Store, the App Store, or the Book Store. To do this:

1   Open either the **iTunes Store**, **App Store** or **Books**

2   For the **App Store** tap on the Account icon and tap on the **Purchased** button; or

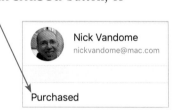

for the **iTunes Store** tap on the **Purchased** button on the bottom toolbar; or
for the **Book Store** tap on the Account icon and view your purchased item under the **My Purchases** heading

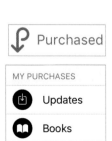

Hot tip

For the iTunes Store, tap on the **My Purchases** button in the Purchased section to access the Family Purchases option; see page 50 for details.

My Purchases

49

...cont'd

3 For all three apps, tap on a member under **Family Purchases** to view their purchases and download them, if required, by tapping once on this button

‹ Account	**All Purchases**	
👤 My Purchases		›
FAMILY PURCHASES		
👤 Eilidh		›

When the Find Friends app is opened, tap on the **Add** button on the top toolbar to add family members. They also have to have Location Services turned **On** (**Settings** > **Privacy** > **Location Services**) so that you can locate them.

Finding family members

Family Sharing makes it easy to keep in touch with the rest of the family and see exactly where they are. This can be done with the Find Friends app. The other person must have their iPad (or other Apple device) turned on and be online. To find family members:

1 Tap on the **Find Friends** app

2 The location of any people who are linked via your Family Sharing is displayed. Tap on a person's name to view their location. Swipe outwards with thumb and forefinger to zoom in on the map

Getting the iPad Online

The iPad is a fun device for listening to music, watching videos and playing games, but to experience the full potential you need to get it online.

Getting online

The fastest connection is Wi-Fi. All iPad models include the Wi-Fi receiver, which means you can browse available wireless networks, choose one and connect.

1 Select **Settings > Wi-Fi**

2 Slide the Wi-Fi slider to **On** if it is **Off**

3 A list of available wireless networks will appear under **Choose a Network.** Tap the one you want to connect to

4 You will likely be prompted for a username and password since most networks are locked (if the network is *open* you will get straight on)

5 Check the signal strength indicator, which will give you an idea of how strong the signal is

Join networks automatically

If this setting is selected, your iPad will connect automatically to wireless networks. This is useful if you move from place to place and have previously joined their network – you will not be prompted each time to re-enter your details. But if you don't want the iPad to join networks automatically, switch this off.

Sometimes you don't want the iPad to remember all used networks (hotels, airports, etc.).

1 Go to **Settings > Wi-Fi** and then select the network you want the iPad to forget

2 Click the right arrow

3 Tap **Forget this Network** and it will be deleted from the list

For a more detailed look at connecting with Wi-Fi see pages 55-56 in Chapter 3.

The iPad may join networks that you don't particularly want to join. Tell it to forget certain networks.

Restore and Reset the iPad

If you are connected to iCloud, your entire iPad contents will be backed up every time you are connected to Wi-Fi.

If the iPad misbehaves, you can reset it and restore it from the iCloud backup. (You can also do this via iTunes if you have backed up your iPad here too.)

Resetting the iPad

There are various options for resetting and restoring your iPad. These are accessed from **Settings** > **General** > **Reset**.

For all of the Reset options there is a confirmation window that needs to be actioned after you have tapped on a specific reset option.

1 Click on the **Reset All Settings** option to return any settings you have applied to their factory defaults. No data or media is deleted with this option

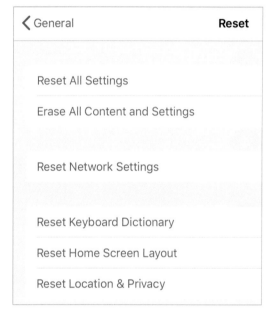

‹ General	Reset
Reset All Settings	
Erase All Content and Settings	
Reset Network Settings	
Reset Keyboard Dictionary	
Reset Home Screen Layout	
Reset Location & Privacy	

Use the **Reset Home Screen Layout** option to return the Home screen to its factory settings.

2 Click on the **Erase All Content and Settings** option to remove everything on your iPad and return it to its factory settings (only do this if you are sure it is backed up). This will erase everything on the iPad

To restore the iPad

If an iPad has been reset with the **Erase All Content and Settings** option, it can be restored when it is turned back on. Select the option for restoring the iPad from the iCloud backup, rather than setting it up as a new device. You will have to enter your Apple ID with which you created your iCloud account, and the iPad will then be restored with the latest backup that was created in iCloud.

If you are selling your iPad, or giving it to someone else, make sure that you use **Erase All Content and Settings** before you hand it over. The new user will then be able to set it up as a new device or from their own iCloud backup.

3 iPad Settings

The whole look and feel of the
iPad is controlled through Settings;
one of the apps pre-installed
on the iPad. In this chapter we
will look at the settings, from
wallpapers to the new feature,
Screen Time, so that you set up
your iPad perfectly for optimal use.

Up in the Air

The iPad is a great multimedia device for listening to music or watching movies on the plane. There are strict rules about wireless and cellular receivers, though – these must be switched off during the flight. Airplane Mode switches all iPad radios off.

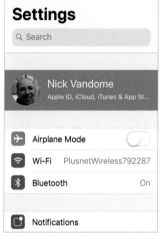
Settings on Wi-Fi model

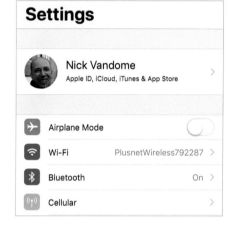
Settings on Wi-Fi + cellular model

Wi-Fi-only models

1   Go to **Settings** > **Wi-Fi**. Turn Wi-Fi **Off** by tapping the **On/Off** button or sliding the slider to the right

2   Wi-Fi is now fully Off. You cannot receive Wi-Fi signals and the iPad is safe to use on the plane

Wi-Fi and cellular models

1   Go to **Settings** > **Airplane Mode** and push the slider to the right

2   Wi-Fi and cellular radios are now fully Off

For both models, when you are off the plane, go back to Settings and slide the slider to the left, which switches the radios back On.

Getting Online with Wi-Fi

The iPad is designed to be used online – using either a wireless connection or cellular network. You can use it without internet access but you won't be able to browse online content, download apps and content, or update your apps.

Connect to a wireless network

1 Open **Settings** > **Wi-Fi**

2 Make sure Wi-Fi is set to **On**

3 Choose a network: you will see a list of available networks near you. If locked (most are) you will see a padlock symbol. Some networks may appear "open" and let you connect but when you browse you will be presented with a request for a username and password

4 Tap the name of the network you want to connect to

5 Enter the password if you know it

6 You should see a check mark next to the network name showing which wireless network you have joined

7 If your network is hidden but you know its name tap **Other...**

8 You can allow the iPad to join networks quietly without alerting you (**Ask to Join Networks – Off**) or you may prefer to be asked before the iPad joins a network (**Ask to Join Networks – On**)

9 You can see the strength of the connection by checking the wireless icon at the top left of the iPad display or in the wireless connection window (in **Settings**)

Hot tip

No Wi-Fi connection? If you have an iPhone, switch on **Personal Hotspot** (**Settings** > **Personal Hotspot**). This lets the iPad use the iPhone's cellular connection. Be careful – the data used comes out of your iPhone allowance!

...cont'd

Setting network connection manually

1 Tap the blue **i** symbol to the right of the network name

2 You can choose an IP address manually or automatically using **Configure IP**, **Subnet Mask** or **Router**. **Configure DNS** is also shown in the window though you won't need to change this

3 If you use a proxy to get onto the internet, enter the details manually or set to **Auto**. Most people don't use proxies so it is unlikely you'll need to change anything here

Don't forget

There is another network setting for switching Bluetooth on or off, for sharing content over short distances with radio connectivity.

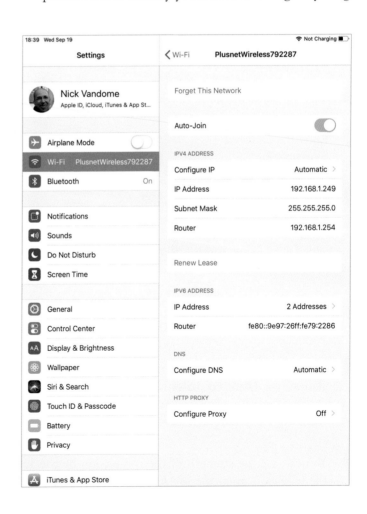

Setting Up Notifications

If you have used the iPhone you will be familiar with notifications. These are audio and visual alerts used by some apps. For example, if you use a messaging app you may want to see how many unread messages there are without actually opening the app. Or, if you use an app like Skype, you may want to be shown on screen when someone is calling you even when the iPad screen is locked. By setting up your notifications you can choose how much or how little information you receive in terms of messages, calls, updates, etc.

Set up notifications

1 Open **Settings** > **Notifications**

2 Under the **Notification Style** heading you will see a list of apps that use notifications

3 To configure notifications for an app, tap its name in the list. You can then turn **On** or **Off** the **Allow Notifications** option and set a sound and style for how these notifications appear in the Notification Center

Some apps offer notification by **Sounds**, **Alerts**, and **Badges**. Sounds **On** means the iPad will play a sound when a notification is received. Alerts are messages that display on the screen, and Badges are the red circles that appear at the top right of the app's icon when notifications have been received.

If you want to keep intrusion from notifications to a minimum, you can adjust the settings on an app-by-app basis.

Notifications can be viewed by swiping down from the left-hand side or middle of any screen. Swipe from right to left to view the available widgets displaying real-time information for items such as weather, calendar and news. Swipe to the bottom of the page and tap on the **Edit** button to change the items that appear on the widgets page.

57

Spend some time setting up your **Notifications** to avoid unwanted intrusions from apps sending useless alerts!

Cellular Data

This is only shown in the combined Wi-Fi and cellular model.

Check cellular data

 Go to **Settings** > **Cellular**

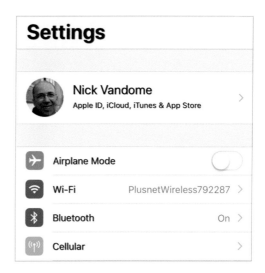

When abroad, keep Data Roaming **Off** or your phone bill may be huge – the cost of data downloaded outside your own country can be very high.

 Make sure Cellular is **On**

You may want to use **Data Roaming** to get online if you are away from your home country. *Note*: Roaming charges for internet access are high so be careful if you switch this to On. In general, it is better to leave this switched Off!

Different carriers will offer specific options and services but some that could be offered include:

- You can view your account, review your data plan, **Add Data** or **Change Plan** (from pay-as-you-go to monthly), and edit user information.

- You can set up a **SIM PIN**.

- Under **SIM Applications** you will see lots of services provided by your cellular carrier.

Set Up Your Wallpaper

Just like your Mac or PC, you can change the picture displayed at the Lock Screen and the background you see behind the apps. You can alter both of these using the in-built iPad wallpapers or you can use your own pictures.

Apple has already provided some excellent images but you may want more. There are several websites offering wallpapers and one of the best is **interfacelift.com**, which offers stunning photos for Mac and PC – these work well on the iPad as well.

Changing the wallpaper

1 Go to **Settings** > **Wallpaper**

2 Tap on the **Choose a New Wallpaper** option

3 Select **Dynamic** or **Stills**, to select a wallpaper, or tap on any of your own photos that are available

4 Tap to make your choice and decide whether you want the new image as only wallpaper or Lock Screen, or both

There are 26 different Apple backgrounds that can be used as wallpaper. These include **Dynamic** backgrounds that appear to move independently from the app's icon layer above, and **Stills** backgrounds.

The **Display & Brightness** setting can be used to change the screen brightness and also change the font size, for apps that support this feature.

Useful Settings

The Settings app has a range of options that can be used to customize your iPad exactly how you want. Some to look at are:

Sounds

This has options to configure the alert sounds for new mail arriving, sent mail, Calendar and social networking app alerts, lock sounds, and keyboard clicks.

Do Not Disturb

This has options for specifying times when calls and notifications are silenced. A specific schedule can be created for this, and allowance made for calls from your favorite contacts.

Screen Time

This can be used to monitor the amount of time spent using the iPad and its apps. To set it up, select **Settings > Screen Time** and tap on the **Turn On Screen Time** button. Tap on the **Continue** button to set up options for: getting a weekly report on your iPad usage; setting limits for how long specific apps can be used; setting restrictions for the type of content that can be viewed; and setting a passcode so that other people cannot override your Screen Time options.

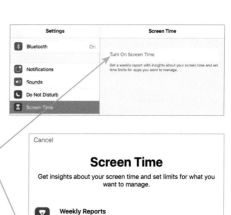

Screen Time is a new feature with iOS 12.

General

This has a range of options for customizing your iPad, such as software updates, multitasking gestures, accessibility, iPad storage, date and time, keyboard options and resetting the iPad.

Control Center

This has options for specifying whether the Control Center can be accessed from within apps and also options for customizing it. See pages 20-21 for details.

Display & Brightness

This has options for changing the iPad's brightness, auto-locking the screen when it is not in use, and also Night Shift, which can be used to specify a schedule for when the color of the display is set to warmer colors, rather than the standard blue light, to aid a good night's sleep.

Siri & Search

This has options for setting up "Hey Siri" for accessing the digital voice assistant (see page 23) and also setting up Siri Shortcuts, whereby an action can be performed by a single trigger word.

Some models of iPad (iPad Air 2 and later, and iPad mini 3 and later) have a Touch ID sensor so that your iPad can only be unlocked by your own unique fingerprint. The setting **Touch ID & Passcode** can be used to set up the Touch ID for the Home button. On other versions of the iPad, the **Passcode** settings can be used to create a 4- or 6-figure passcode for unlocking your iPad. The latest models of the iPad Pro (announced October 2018) use Face ID rather than Touch ID.

Privacy

This can be used to turn on Location Services for the iPad and also specific apps, so that your location can be identified when in use, to provide additional functionality.

Wallet & Apple Pay

This can be used to authorize credit and debit cards for use with Apple Pay – Apple's method of contactless payment. It can also be used to set up Apple Pay Cash, for paying individuals using the Messages apps (only in certain locations).

Passwords & Accounts

This can be used to view stored passwords and also add additional accounts; i.e. if you want to add a Google account so that you can receive Google Mail emails in the Mail app.

Apple Pay Cash (where available) can be set up in the Wallet & Apple Pay settings by dragging the **Apple Pay Cash** button to **On** and following the setup process. The Messages app can then be used to send money to other people by tapping on this button.

61

Mail, Contacts, Calendars

These are three separate settings that enable you to manage your email accounts, your contacts, and your calendars.

Mail

Preview – how many lines of the email do you want to preview?

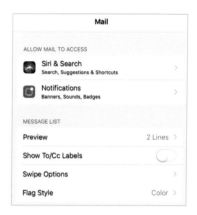

Show To/Cc Labels – show or hide this option.

Swipe Options – tap on this for options for what appears when you swipe left or right on an email in your Inbox.

Flag Style – this determines the color and shape of flags that are used on emails.

Ask Before Deleting – switch to **On** as a safety measure, preventing the unwanted deletion of emails.

Load Remote Images – if an email contains images and you want to see these, switch to **On**.

Organize By Thread – drag this **On** to view email conversations combined into individual threads.

Collapse Read Messages – this is used to collapse a read message into its thread.

Most Recent Message on Top – this displays the most recent message at the top of the thread.

Complete Threads – this displays all of the messages in a thread, even if some have been moved to another mailbox.

Always Bcc Myself – for blind copies sent to yourself.

Mark Addresses – use this to add flags to certain types of email addresses.

Increase Quote Level – this indents messages that you forward to people.

Signature – assign a signature for the end of each email.

Hot tip

New email accounts can be set up within **Settings** > **Passwords & Accounts** by tapping on the **Add Account** button.

Contacts

Sort Order – sort your contacts by first or last name.

Display Order – same as above.

Short Name – select the format for abbreviated names.

My Info – view your own details within the **Contacts** app.

Calendars

Time Zone Override – switch to **Off** to display events for your current location.

Alternate Calendars – select calendars for different languages.

Week Numbers – turn **On** to show week numbers for the current year, at the start of the week.

Show Invitee Declines – show any declined calendar invites.

Sync – set a timescale for syncing your calendar events.

Default Alert Times – set alert times for certain events.

Start Week On – set a day for your calendar to start on.

Default Calendar – select the default calendar for new events.

Location Suggestions – this can be used to suggest locations when events are added to the calendar.

The Siri & Search option in the Mail, Contacts and Calendars settings can be used to display results from Siri when you search for a keyword or phrase that relates to content in one of these apps. Tap on the **Siri & Search** option and drag the **Siri & Suggestions** button On to activate this for each app.

63

Safari and Media Settings

Search Engine – select Google, Yahoo!, Bing, or DuckDuckGo.

Search Engine Suggestions – use this to display suggestions as you type into the Address Bar or a search engine.

Safari Suggestions – use this to display suggestions as you type into the Spotlight Search box.

Quick Website Search – turn this **On** to use the Smart Search Field for searching using a website name and then a specific keyword, to search for it on the selected website.

Preload Top Hit – use this to enable Safari to start loading the top result from a search, to make it quicker to access it.

AutoFill – can be used to remember your passwords and details entered into forms.

Frequently Visited Sites – this can be used to display your most visited sites when you open a new tab or web page.

Favorites – use this for what is displayed on the Favorites page, when you open a new tab or enter an address in the Address Bar.

Open New Tabs in Background – use this if you want to open new tabs while you are still viewing the current page.

Show Favorites Bar – use this to show or hide the Favorites Bar (this is displayed at the top of the Safari window).

Show Tab Bar – use this to show all open tabs on the Tab Bar, just below the Favorites Bar.

Show Icons in Tabs – turn this **On** to show websites' icons on open tabs.

Block Pop-ups – leave **On** to avoid annoying pop-ups.

Prevent Cross-Site Tracking – turn this **On** to prevent websites from tracking your activity from one site to another.

Block Cookies – many sites insist on allowing cookies but you can clear all the cookies (see Clear History and Website Data).

Ask Websites Not to Track Me – turn this **On** to prevent websites from tracking your online activity.

AutoFill is useful and saves you having to type your personal details into website forms. However, do not use it if other people have access to your iPad.

64

Showing icons on open tabs is a new feature in iOS 12.

Fraudulent Website Warning – it is wise to be alerted when you visit potentially fraudulent sites so leave this **On**.

Camera & Microphone Access – gives websites access to the iPad's camera and microphone.

Check for Apple Pay – checks a website to see if it accepts Apple Pay for payment on the site.

Clear History and Website Data – tap on this to delete details of your web browsing history and stored website data.

Automatically Save Offline – use this to save Reading List items so that they can be read offline.

Advanced – a range of advanced settings, such as using JavaScript.

Maps

Preferred Transportation Type – select a default option for how directions are displayed on maps, for driving, walking or transit.

Distances – choose to display distances in kilometers or miles.

Map Labels – turn labels in English **On** or **Off**.

Music

Show Apple Music – turn this **On** to view the Apple Music option within the Music app. This is a subscription service that provides access to the full music catalogue in the iTunes Library.

Join Apple Music – use this to join Apple Music, the online music subscription service. This can also be done from the Music app itself.

Download Music – this determines the default of how content is displayed in the Music app.

Playback – this includes settings for a graphic equalizer (**EQ**), **Volume Limit** and **Sound Check**.

Home Sharing Sign In – use this to share items from iTunes with other devices within your home, on the same network.

The **Notes** and **Reminders** apps also have their own settings.

There is a range of **Privacy** settings where you can turn on **Location Services** so that specific apps can use your current geographic location.

The **Battery** settings can be used to display the remaining amount of battery power on the iPad's status bar and also how much battery usage each app is consuming.

...cont'd

TV

Playback Quality – select the quality for playing content from the iTunes Store. The options are **Best Available** and **Good**.

Purchases and Rentals – select the default options for downloading content from the iTunes Store. The options are **High Definition** or **Standard Definition**.

Photos

Sharing options – select options for sharing your photos to your own devices with iCloud and your Photo Stream (for more details, see Chapter 6, page 93).

Photos Tab – turn this **On** or **Off** to show or hide summaries of your photos.

Camera

Preserve Settings – use this to keep the most recently-used camera setting; e.g. if Slo-Mo was the most recently used, it will be available as the default the next time you open the camera.

Grid – use this to turn a grid **On** or **Off** for the camera, to help with composing photos.

Record Video/Slo-mo – options for the quality of these two recording functions.

High Dynamic Range (HDR) – use this to blend the best exposures from three photos, while keeping the originals too.

iTunes & App Store

This is where you set up your account details for the iTunes and App Store.

Tap on the account name to see your details, including address, phone number and credit card.

Automatic Downloads – select which items out of Music, Apps, Books & Audiobooks and Updates you want to be downloaded automatically, when you are connected to online services over Wi-Fi.

There are also settings for social networking sites, including Facebook and Twitter, that enable you to log in to these accounts and link them to iOS 12, if they have been added on your iPad.

FaceTime settings can also be used to add email addresses that can be used for video or audio chatting. There is also an option to disable FaceTime for calls.

4 Browsing the Web

Browsing the web is probably the most popular activity on desktop and laptop computers, so it comes as no surprise that the same is true of the iPad. Safari is pre-installed on the iPad and is a clean, fast browser that will more than satisfy all of your browsing needs.

Around Safari

The Safari app is the default web browser on the iPad. This can be used to view web pages, save Favorites and read pages with the Reader function. To start using Safari:

1 Tap on the **Safari** app

2 Tap on the Address Bar at the top of the Safari window. Type a web page address

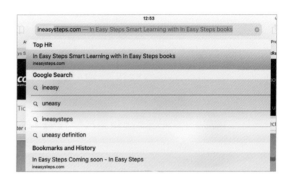

3 Tap on the **Go** button on the keyboard to open the web page, or select one of the suggested options below the Address Bar

4 The selected page opens with the top toolbar visible. As you scroll down the page this disappears to give you a greater viewing area. Tap on the top of the screen or scroll back up to display the toolbar again

When you type in the Safari Address Bar, the Favorites window appears from where you can select one of your Favorite or Bookmarked web pages.

68

When a page opens in Safari, a blue status bar underneath the page name indicates the progress of the loading page.

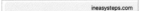

Navigating Pages

When you are viewing pages within Safari there are a number of functions that can be used:

1 Tap on these buttons to move forward and back between web pages that have been visited

2 Tap here to view bookmarked pages, Reading List pages and History

3 Tap here to add a bookmark, add to a Reading List, add an icon to your iPad Home screen, email a link to a page, share via social media or print a page

4 Tap here to add a new tab

5 Tap on a link on a page to open it. Tap and hold to access additional options, to open in a new tab, add to a Reading List or copy the link

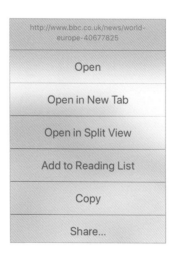

6 Tap and hold on an image and tap on **Save Image** or **Copy**

Tap and hold on the **Forward** and **Back** buttons to view lists of previously-visited pages in these directions.

The **Reading List** is similar to Bookmarks and you can use it to save pages that you want to read later. Also, you can read them when you are offline. The Reading List can be accessed from the button in Step 2.

Opening New Tabs

Safari supports tabbed browsing, which means that you can open separate pages within the same window and access them by tapping on each tab at the top of the page:

1 Tap here to open a new tab for another web page

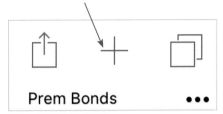

The items that appear in the Favorites window can be determined within **Settings** > **Safari** by tapping on the **Favorites** link.

2 Open a new page by entering a web address into the Address Bar, or tap on one of the thumbnails in the **Favorites** window

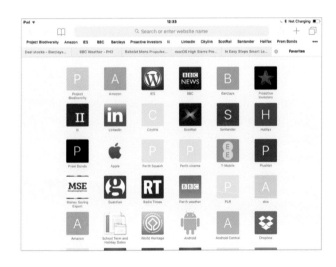

3 Tap on the tab headings to move between tabbed pages

If there are too many items to be displayed on the Favorites Bar, tap on this button to view the other items.

4 Tap on the cross at the top of a tab to close it

Tab View

This functionality gives you the ability to view all of your open Safari tabs on one screen. To use this:

1 Tap here to activate Tab View

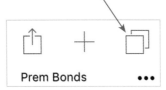

2 All of the currently-open tabs are displayed. Tap on one to open it

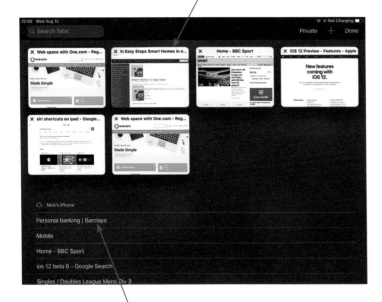

3 If you have open Safari tabs on other Apple devices, these will be shown at the bottom of the window

4 Tap on this button at the top of the window to open another tab

5 Tap on this button to open a **Private** tab, from where no browsing record will be recorded during the browsing session

Hot tip

Tab View can also be activated by pinching inwards with thumb and forefinger on a web page that is at normal magnification; i.e. 1 to 1.

71

Don't forget

Tap on the **Done** button at the top of the Tab View window to exit this and return to the web page that was being viewed when Tab View was activated.

Bookmarking Pages

Once you start using Safari you will soon build up a collection of favorite pages that you visit regularly. To access these quickly they can be bookmarked, so that you can then go to them in one tap. To set up and use Bookmarks:

1 Open a web page that you want to bookmark. Tap here to access the sharing options

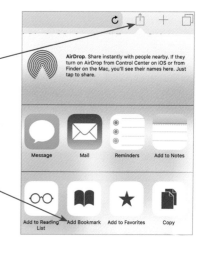

2 Tap on the **Add Bookmark** button

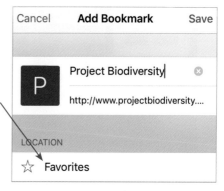

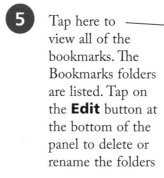

The Favorites Bar appears underneath the Address Bar in Safari. This includes items that have been added as Bookmarks.

3 Tap on this link and select whether to include the bookmark on the Favorites Bar or in a Bookmarks folder

4 Tap on the **Save** button

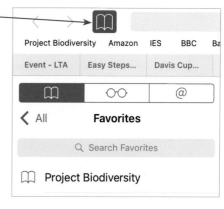

5 Tap here to view all of the bookmarks. The Bookmarks folders are listed. Tap on the **Edit** button at the bottom of the panel to delete or rename the folders

Safari History

All of your web browsing will leave a history trail behind. This is useful if you want to revisit sites (*you should have saved a bookmark!*). Over time, the history list will become huge so it's a good idea to clear this from time to time. In addition, other people using your iPad can see your history, and there may be sites you visit that you would prefer to keep private!

Clear the history

1 Go to **Settings** > **Safari**

2 Tap **Clear History and Website Data**

3 You will be asked to confirm this action

4 Tap **Clear** and the history will be cleared

If you clear your history and website data, Safari will not remember any websites that you have visited or any other items from sites, so it will not be able to suggest website names when you start entering them into the Address Bar.

Add Links to Home Screen

The various iPad screens are home to all of your apps, but you can also add web pages as buttons to the Home screen, to make finding and opening these easier. You wouldn't want all of your saved websites to be added to the Home screen or you would have very little room for actual apps. But for websites that are very important, or that you visit regularly, consider adding them to the Home screen.

1 Navigate to a site you want to save

2 Tap the **Share** icon

3 Choose **Add to Home Screen**

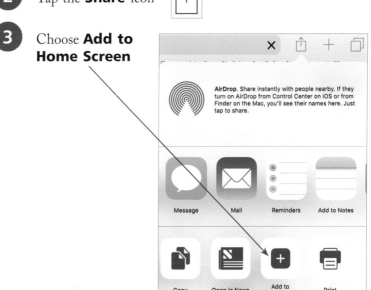

Hot tip

You can also share web page links to the Notes app. This creates a note with a link to the required website.

74

4 Name the saved link and tap on the **Add** button

5 The web page will resemble an app on the Home screen

6 Tap it and it will open Safari and take you straight to the correct web page

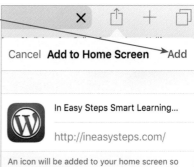

Safari Privacy

We have already looked at the history and clearing this from time to time. The other item worth clearing on the iPad (and regular computer browsers, for that matter) is the Cookies file. This is a file containing sites you have visited, and the entries are made by the sites themselves. They don't necessarily do any major harm, but for reasons of privacy it is a good idea to clear Cookies periodically.

1 Go to **Settings > Safari >** and tap on **Block All Cookies**

2 To confirm the action, tap on **Block All**

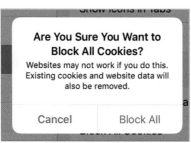

Other privacy settings can also be applied, to try to prevent websites tracking your actions and to warn you about the possibility of fraudulent websites:

1 Drag **On** the **Prevent Cross-Site Tracking** button to stop websites tracking your actions from site to site and sharing your browsing information with them

2 Drag **On** the **Ask Websites Not to Track Me** button to prevent websites tracking your actions

3 Drag **On** the **Fraudulent Website Warning** button to be alerted to websites that are not all that they seem and that may have security issues

For peace of mind, clear Cookies and History from time to time, as described on page 73.

Web tracking can be useful for a website to build up a profile of your preferences for when you next visit the site, but it can also mean that they have a lot of information that could be used for other purposes, such as sending you a range of marketing material.

Other Web Browsers

Safari is the default pre-installed browser on the iPad but there are others, which include:

- Opera Mini (*shown below*).

- Firefox.

- Private Browsing.

- Dolphin Web Browser.

- Web Browser (Free).

- iWeb.

Some of these are written specifically for the iPad, while others are for the iPhone but can be used on the iPad.

What are the advantages of using third-party browsers?

- Many offer private browsing (no history retained).

- If you get bored with Safari and fancy a change, try out one of these other ones and see if it suits your needs better.

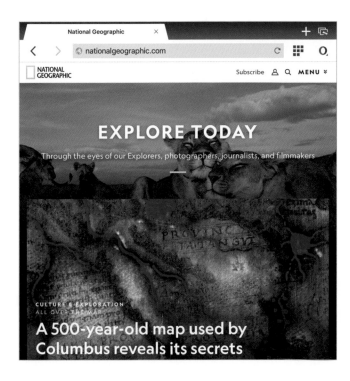

5 Mail, Text and FaceTime

Love it or loathe it, email is a fact of life. We need to deal with email both at work and at home. Mail on the iPad makes reading and sending emails a pleasure, and in this chapter we will look at how to set up your accounts, manage your Inbox, and make the most of IMAP email. Also covered is the Messages app for sending text messages, which can be enhanced with a variety of items.

What is Mail?

Some of us spend much of our time on PCs and Macs checking and sending emails. This is also true of mobile devices like the iPhone and other handhelds. So, not surprisingly, a fair amount of your time on the iPad may be spent doing emails.

The Mail app built in to the iPad is a feature-rich program that is easy to set up and use. It is similar to Mail, which comes with every MacBook and Mac desktop, although a few features are lacking. There's no stationery option on the iPad version, and you can't have multiple signatures.

Setting up an email account

1 Go to **Settings > Passwords & Accounts** and tap on the **Add Account** link

2 You will see a list of options

3 Choose the one that matches your email account

4 If you can't see it, select **Other** – enter your details including email address and password. The program will work out the rest for you

POP or IMAP?

For most people these are fairly confusing terms but it's worth having a look at both types before setting your accounts up. POP stands for *Post Office Protocol* and IMAP means *Internet Message Access Protocol*. These are the two most common standards for email retrieval. POP3 is the current version of POP, and is used for web-based email such as Google Mail. Rather than look at the nuts and bolts of these two systems, we can summarize the pros and cons of each.

For Mail, IMAP email offers many advantages over POP3.

IMAP lets you see all of your emails using any machine

If you use multiple computers – including handhelds such as the iPad – IMAP allows you to see your various mail folders from any device. The folder structure and the emails within the folders are the same because the folders and emails are kept on a central server (*not* on your computer or iPad).

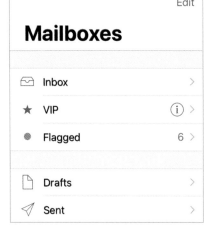

When you set up a POP3 account you will see folders for Inbox, Sent Mail, and Trash, but no sub-folders or the opportunity to create sub-folders to categorize and file your emails. But with an IMAP account you can create as many folders and sub-folders as you like, and file all of your emails. You can browse all of your IMAP folders and emails on the iPad and transfer new emails into their respective folders, just as you would with paper mail using a file cabinet. There is a downside to IMAP, though – since the emails are stored on a server that may be in the US (iCloud emails are currently stored in California), if you have no internet connection you may not be able to see your emails.

So, which should you use?

If your email provider – e.g. Apple (iCloud) – provides IMAP then select that. If POP3 is the only option you have, there's not much you can do to change this. For those of us wishing to archive emails and retrieve them months or years later, IMAP is the best possible solution.

Composing an Email

To compose an email with the Mail app:

1 Open **Mail** by tapping its icon, and decide which account you want to use (if you have more than one) by tapping **Accounts** and choosing one

2 Tap the **New email** icon

3 Enter the name of the recipient. As you start typing, Mail will present you with a list of possible options. Choose the recipient from the list if it is there

4 Tap the **Subject** box and enter the email subject here

5 Tap the main body of the email and type the text of your email

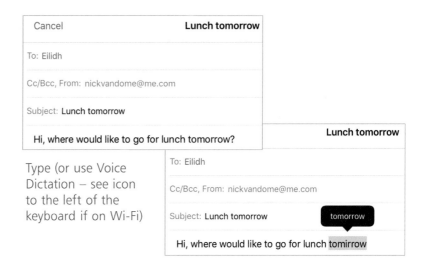

Type (or use Voice Dictation – see icon to the left of the keyboard if on Wi-Fi)

Mail will spot mistakes and suggest the correct word.

6 If you want to copy someone in on the email, use the **Cc** box. To send a blind copy (the primary email recipient cannot see that a blind copy has been sent to another person, hence the term "blind"), tap the **Bcc** box

7 Check the **spelling** – any errors will be underlined with a red dotted line. Correct by tapping on the misspelled word and choosing from available options, or delete the word and retype if Mail does not offer the correct word

8 Once you're happy with the content and spelling, tap **Send** and your email will be sent

Attach files to an email

At present you cannot attach files in the same way as you would with a regular computer – there's no real "desktop" or filing system you can see in order to find and attach a file. However, it can be done by pressing and holding within an email – see tip.

You can also send files such as documents and photos by sharing via email from *within* an app.

For example, in the Photos app there is an option to share photos by email. You can email Safari web pages from within the Safari app, and document management programs like Documents To Go allow you to email files from within the Documents To Go app.

Hot tip

You can add a photo or a video directly into an email by pressing and holding in the body of the email and tapping on the **Insert Photo or Video** button. You can then select the required item from the Photos app.

81

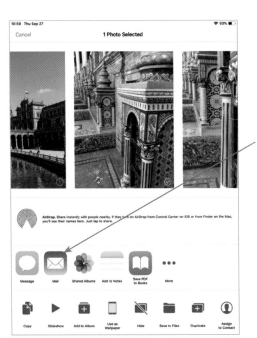

Here, a photo has been opened in Photos. To email the photo, tap the **Share** button and select **Mail** from the options.

This option can be found in many apps on the iPad.

Receiving and Reading Emails

Emails are "pushed" through to the iPad from the email server if your iPad is online. You can tell there are unread emails by looking for the badge on the app's icon.

Manually checking for email
You can make Mail check for new email by pulling down on the email list.

Reading emails in portrait mode
If you hold the iPad in portrait mode you will see a separate, floating account window, listing emails in the Inbox.

1 Tap an email in the list and it will fill the whole screen

2 To see the next or previous email, tap the up or down arrows ∧ ∨ or tap Inbox again. Next to the word **Inbox** you may see (3), which means you have three unread emails in the Inbox

3 When reading emails you can: **Move** the email ▱, **Delete** 🗑, **Reply or Reply All** ↩, **Forward** the email to someone else (press on this button and tap on Forward) ↩, **Compose** a new email ✎ and **Flag** an email ⚑

Reading emails in landscape mode

1 Tap the email you want to read – it will be displayed in the right-hand pane

2 If you want to navigate to other folders in your account, tap the name of the account (top left) and you will see a folder list

3 Scroll up or down until you find the folder you want, then tap it. You will then see the emails contained within that folder

Hot tip

Manual send and receive will save power. It is also the best way to retrieve email if you are using Data Roaming. To turn off Push, go to **Settings** > **Password & Accounts** > **Fetch New Data** and drag the **Push** button to **Off**.

4 Navigate back up the hierarchy by tapping the previous location link at the top

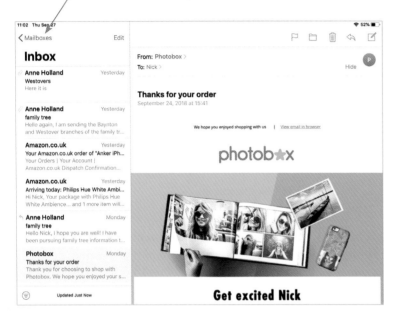

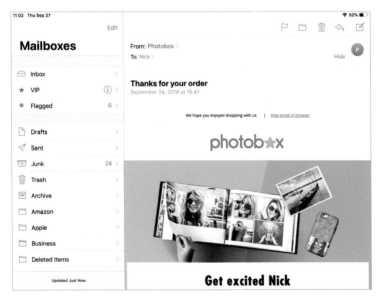

Searching for Emails

Mail provides a simple Search box at the top left, below the account name. You can search: **From**, **To**, **Subject**, **All**.

Searching for emails is usually quicker than looking for them manually.

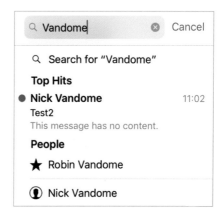

Searching for emails across multiple accounts
You can also search for emails using the Spotlight search:

1 Go to **Spotlight** search (press and hold on an empty space on a Home screen and swipe downwards)

2 Enter your search terms into the Search box

3 Spotlight will then search all of your emails (and also Calendars, Contacts, Music, etc. unless you have configured Spotlight so it only searches emails)

4 Once the email you are looking for is listed in the search list, tap it and Mail will open, and take you to that email open on the screen

Deleting Unwanted Emails

We all receive email spam or emails we don't want to keep. It's easy to delete emails, either singly or in batches.

Delete a single email

1 If the email you want to delete is open on the screen, simply tap the **Trash** icon and the email will be sent to the Trash folder

2 If you are looking at a list of emails in the account window, tap **Edit** then tap the radio button next to the email you want to delete. Then hit **Trash**. The numbers in brackets tell you that one email has been selected for Delete or Move

3 Another way of deleting emails is to view the list in the account window then drag your finger across the email from right to left and a **Trash** button will appear. Tap this and the email will be deleted

Hot tip

Tap on the **More** button in Step 3 to access more options, including moving the email to Junk. Tap on the **Flag** button to add a flag to the email, to make it easier to find.

85

Don't forget

Deleted emails can usually be salvaged from the Trash if you want to recover them. Within the Trash folder, look down the list for emails you want to recover from the Trash. Tap **Edit** and tap the **radio button** of the email you want to recover. Tap **Move** and choose **Inbox**. The message will move from Trash to Inbox.

Adding Mailboxes

Different categories of email messages can be managed via Mailboxes. For instance, you may want to keep your social emails separately from ones that apply to financial activities.

Hot tip

Messages can be edited within individual mailboxes. To do this, select a mailbox and tap on the **Edit** button. The message can then be edited with the **Delete**, **Move**, or **Mark** options at the bottom of the window.

Don't forget

Emails can be organized into specific folders. To do this, with the email open, tap the **Folder** icon:

Decide which folder you want to use to store the email.

Tap on the folder name and the email will move across into its new location.

Move back to the main account level and tap on the folder name to view its contents.

1 From your Inbox, tap on the **Mailboxes** button

2 The current mailboxes are displayed. Tap on **Edit**

Edit

Edit

Mailboxes

✉ Inbox		›
★ VIP	ⓘ	›
⚑ Flagged	6	›
📎 Attachments		›
📄 Drafts		›
✈ Sent		›

3 Tap on **New Mailbox** at the bottom of the Mailboxes panel

New Mailbox

4 Enter a name for the new mailbox. Tap on the **Save** button

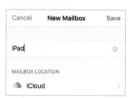
Cancel   New Mailbox   Save
iPad
MAILBOX LOCATION
☁ iCloud

5 Tap on the **Done** button   Done

6 To delete a mailbox, tap on it, then tap on the **Delete Mailbox** button

Cancel   Edit Mailbox   Save
iPad
MAILBOX LOCATION
☁ iCloud
Delete Mailbox

Messaging

On your iPad you can join the world of text with the Apple iMessage service that is accessed via the Messages app. This enables text, photo, video, emojis, and audio messages to be sent, free of charge, between users of iOS on the iPad, iPhone, iPod Touch and Mac computers. iMessages can be sent to cell/mobile phone numbers and email addresses. To use Messages:

1 Tap on the **Messages** app

2 Tap on this button to create a new message and start a new conversation

3 Tap on this button to select someone from your contacts

4 Tap on a contact to select them as the recipient of the new message

Groups	Contacts	Cancel
Q Search		
E		
Paul **Eddy**		A
		•
Eilidh		D
		•

5 Tap in the text box, and type with the keyboard to create a message. Tap on this button to send the message

New iMessage   Cancel

To: Eilidh,   ⊕

📷 Ⓐ Hello, how are you?| ↑

You need an Apple ID to send iMessages.

iMessages are sent using Wi-Fi. If a Wi-Fi connection is not available, the message cannot be sent unless the iPad has a cellular network connection.

If an iPad has a cellular network connection then this can be used to send regular text messages to other compatible devices such as cell/mobile phones. If the recipient is not using iMessages, the message will be sent as a standard SMS (Short Message Service). By default, iMessages appear in blue bubbles and SMS messages in green bubbles.

...cont'd

6 As the conversation progresses, each message is displayed in the main window

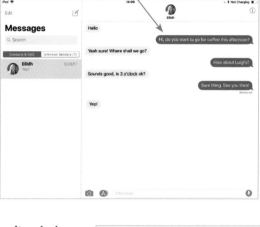

Hot tip

Press and hold on a message, and tap on the **More...** button that appears. Select a message, or messages, and tap on the **Trash** icon to remove them.

7 To edit whole conversations, tap on the **Edit** button in the Messages panel

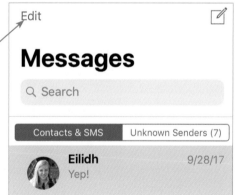

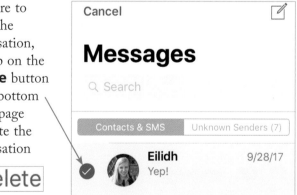

Don't forget

When a message has been sent, you are notified underneath it when it has been delivered.

8 Tap here to select the conversation, and tap on the **Delete** button at the bottom of the page to delete the conversation

Enhancing Text Messages

Adding emojis

Emojis (small graphical symbols) are now very common in text messages, and can easily be included with iOS 12. To use these:

1 Tap on this button on the keyboard to view the emoji keyboards

2 Swipe left and right to view the emoji options. Tap on an emoji to add it to a message

Message effects

iMessages can also be sent with certain animated effects:

1 Write a message and press on this button

2 Tap on the **Bubble** button at the top of the window, and tap on one of the options. These are **Slam**, which creates a message that moves in at speed from the side of the screen; **Loud**, which creates a message in large text; **Gentle**, which creates a message in small text; and **Invisible Ink**, which creates a message that is concealed and then reveals the text

3 Repeat Step 1 for Bubble effects above and tap on the **Screen** button at the top of the window. Swipe left and right to view the full-screen effects

4 Tap on this button next to the text box to display the App Strip underneath

5 Tap on the **Photos** button in the App Strip to include photos in a message and tap on the **Store** button to download sticker sets from the App Store

The range of emojis has been expanded with iOS 12.

Beware

The effects on this page require the recipient to be using iMessages and iOS 10, or later. If not, they may appear differently, or may not have the same animated effects.

Hot tip

Handwritten messages can also be created. Tap on this button on the keyboard to access the handwriting panel. Write using your finger or an Apple Pencil and tap on the **Done** button to add it to a message. The text appears animated to the recipient.

Using FaceTime

Video chatting is a very personal and interactive way to keep in touch with family and friends around the world. The FaceTime app provides this facility to video chat with other users of Apple devices. To use FaceTime for video chatting:

1 Tap on the **FaceTime** app

2 Recent video chats are shown in the left-hand panel. Tap on a previous caller, or tap here to create a new call

Don't forget

A FaceTime call is connected once a recipient has been selected. The recipient then has to accept the call. Once this has been done, the recipient's video feed appears in the main window, and your own video feed appears in a thumbnail window in the top left-hand corner.

3 Tap here to select a recipient from your Contacts app

4 Once a call has been connected, tap on this button for call options

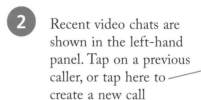

5 Tap on the top line of buttons to, from left to right: mute the call; end the call; or change the camera view from back to front. Tap on the bottom line of buttons to, from left to right: send a text message; put the call on speaker; or turn the camera off

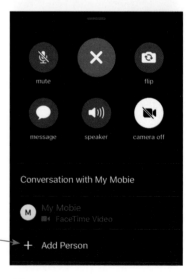

NEW

Group FaceTime is a new feature in iOS 12.

6 Tap on the **Add Person** button to add more people to the call. This is known as Group FaceTime

6 Photos

The Photos iPad app delivers rich-looking photos at high resolution so you can view all of your albums as slideshows, or share them with family and friends.

Taking Photos and Videos

Because of its mobility and the quality of the screen, the iPad is excellent for taking and displaying photos. Photos can be captured directly using one of the two built-in cameras (one on the front and one on the back) and then viewed, edited and shared using the Photos app. To do this:

1 Tap on the **Camera** app

2 Tap on this button to capture a photo (or press the volume button at the side of the iPad)

3 Tap on this button to swap between the front or back cameras on the iPad

Hot tip

Tap on the HDR (High Dynamic Range) button to take three versions of the same subject that will then be blended into a single photo, using the best exposures from each photo.

The iPad cameras can be used for different formats and functions:

1 Swipe up or down at the side of the camera screen, underneath the shutter button, to access the different shooting options. Tap on the **Photo** button to capture photos at full-screen size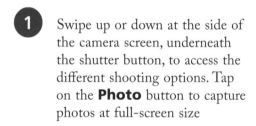

2 Tap on the **Square** button to capture photos at this ratio

3 Tap on the **Video** button and press the red shutter button to take a video

4 Tap on this button to take a **Live Photo** when the shutter button is tapped. A Live Photo is a short animated image that captures a short period of time before and after the shutter button is tapped, to create the animated effect. Live Photos can be viewed in the Photos app by tapping on them

Hot tip

Tap on these buttons on the main toolbar to, from top to bottom: take a photo with a self-timer of either 3 or 10 seconds; turn the flash on or off; or select Auto.

Photos and Camera Settings

iCloud sharing

Certain camera options can be applied within Settings. Several of these are to do with storing and sharing your photos via iCloud. To access these:

1 Tap on the **Settings** app

2 Tap on the **Photos** tab

3 Drag the **iCloud Photos** button to **On** to upload

 iCloud Photos

your whole iPad photo library to the iCloud (it remains on your iPad too). Similarly, photos on your other Apple devices can also be uploaded to the iCloud and these will then be available on your iPad as well

4 Select an option for storing iCloud

Optimize iPad Storage ✓

Download and Keep Originals

photos. **Optimize iPad Storage** uses less storage, as it uses device-optimized versions of your images; i.e. smaller file sizes

5 Drag the **My Photo Stream** button to **On** to

 My Photo Stream

enable all new photos and videos that you take on your iPad to be uploaded automatically to the iCloud

6 Drag the **Shared Albums** button to **On** to allow you

 Shared Albums

to create albums within the Photos app that can then be shared with other people via iCloud

If the **iCloud Photos** option is **On** then your photos will all appear in the **All Photos** album in the Albums section, as well as in the Photos section. If iCloud Photo Library is **Off** there will be a **Camera Roll** album in the Albums section, where photos created on your iPad will appear.

Drag the **Grid** button in the **Camera** app to On to place a grid over the screen when you are taking photos with the camera, if required. This can be used to help compose photos by placing subjects using the grid.

Getting Photos onto the iPad

Because of its high-resolution display and rich colors, the iPad is perfect for viewing photos. The iPad supports pictures in a number of formats including JPEG, TIFF, GIF, and PNG. But how do you get your photos onto the iPad in the first place, in addition to using either of the two iPad cameras?

Importing from a computer program

1 You can import from Aperture on the Mac or from photo-editing software such as Adobe Photoshop Elements

2 Connect the iPad to your Mac and use iTunes to configure which albums you want to sync and also remove from selected albums

Using a Lightning to SD Card Camera Reader

1 Plug in the Lightning to SD Card Camera Reader

2 Insert the SD card from your camera

3 Click **Import Photos**

4 You will be asked whether you want to keep or delete the photos on the SD card

5 View your photos by tapping the **Photos** app

Using a Lightning to USB Camera Adapter

1 Plug the Lightning to USB Camera Adapter into the iPad

2 Attach the camera using the camera cable

3 Make sure the camera is turned **On** and is in Transfer mode

4 Select the photos you want to import

Hot tip

If photos are taken on an iPhone, they can be viewed automatically on an iPad using iCloud. See page 93 for the relevant sharing settings.

Don't forget

A Lightning to SD card Camera Reader connects to the iPad's Lightning port and the camera's SD card is inserted into the card reader, so that the photos can be imported onto the iPad.

Don't forget

When importing photos from a camera you can also choose whether to keep the photos on the camera once they have been imported, or delete them.

Adding Photos from Email

You can email a photo to yourself to open and download to your iPad, or add any photos you have received in an email in the same way.

1 Open the email containing the photo or image

2 Make sure you can see the image you want to import then tap and hold your finger on the image until you see a pop-up including **Message**, **Mail**, **Notes**, **Twitter**, **Facebook**, **Flickr**, **iCloud Photo Sharing**, **Quick Look**, **Save Image**, **Markup and Reply**, **Assign to Contact**, **Copy** and **Print**

3 Tap **Save Image** and the image will be sent to the **Photos** app on the iPad

Hot tip

Tap on the **Notes** option in Step 2 to create a new item in the **Notes** app, with the photo inserted.

95

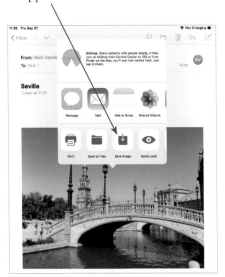

Saving photos or images from Safari web pages

1 Tap and hold your finger on the image you want to save, until you see a pop-up

2 Tap the **Save Image** option

3 The image will be sent to the **Photos** app on the iPad

Viewing Photos

Once photos have been captured, they can be viewed and organized in the Photos app. To do this:

1 Tap on the **Photos** app

The layout of the Photos app has been updated in iOS 12.

2 Tap on the **Photos** button on the bottom toolbar

Hot tip

If you have iCloud set up, all of your photos will also be saved under the **All Photos** album in the **Albums** section. This enables all of your photos to be made available on any other devices you have with iCloud, such as an iPhone, an iPod Touch or a Mac computer.

3 At the top level, all photos are displayed according to the years in which they were taken

4 Tap on images to view them in more detail by date taken. Tap once on the Back arrow to move back a level

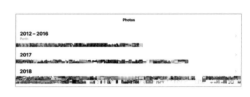

5 Tap (or double-tap, depending on the view level) on a thumbnail photo to view it at full size

Hot tip

Double-tap with one finger on an individual photo to zoom in on it. Double-tap with one finger again to zoom back out. To zoom in to a greater degree, swipe outwards with thumb and forefinger.

6 Swipe with one finger or drag here to move through all of the available photos

For You Tab

In Photos app the For You section is where the best of your photos are selected and displayed automatically. To use this:

1 Tap on the **For You** button on the bottom toolbar of the Photos app

2 Memories are displayed in the For You section. These are collections of photos created by the Photos app, using what it determines are the best shots for a related series of photos

The For You tab is a new feature in the Photos app in iOS 12.

3 Albums are displayed below the Memories. These include albums that have been shared with, and by, other people

4 Tap on a Memory in Step 2 to view its details. The top panel displays a slideshow of the photos, which are also displayed below. Tap on the **Play** button to view a full-screen slideshow of all of the images, including music

When a Memory is playing a full-screen slideshow as shown in Step 4, tap on an image on the screen and tap on the **Edit** button, in the top right-hand corner to access the editing options for the Memory. These include editing the music, title, duration and the items in the Memory. Tap on the **Done** button in the bottom right-hand corner to exit the editing mode.

Creating Albums

Within the Photos app it is possible to create different albums in which you can store photos. This can be a good way to organize them according to different categories and headings. To do this:

When photos are placed into albums, the originals remain in the main **Photos** section. Any changes to the photos in the album will not affect the originals in Photos.

1 Tap on the **Albums** button

2 Tap on this button

3 Select the type of album that you want to create

4 Enter a name for the new album and tap on the **Save** button

New Album
Enter a name for this album.

Zoo

Cancel   Save

5 Tap on the photos you want to include in the album

6 Tap on the **Done** button

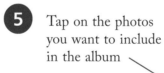

Done

Add 4 photos to "Zoo".

7 The new album is added to the Albums section in the Photos app

Selecting Photos

It is easy to take hundreds or thousands of digital photos, and most of the time you will only want to use a selection of them. Within the Photos app it is possible to select individual photos so that you can share them, delete them or add them to albums.

1   Access one of the photos views and tap on the **Select** button

2   Tap on the photos you want to select, or tap on the **Select** button again to select all of the photos

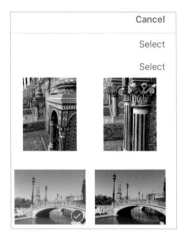

3   Tap on the **Deselect** button if you want to remove the selection

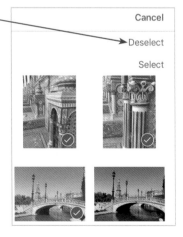

Tap on the **Share** button in Step 4 to access an option to copy a selected photo.

Hot tip

4   Use these buttons to, from left to right: share the selected photos, delete them or add them to an album

Photos Slideshow

All or some of your photos in the Photos app can be viewed in a continuous slideshow, and you can even add your own music to it. To do this:

1 Tap an **Album** to open it

2 Tap the **Slideshow** button (if you can't see the controls, tap the screen)

3 Tap on the screen and tap on the **Options** button on the bottom toolbar. Tap on the **Music** button to select a song from the music library (or select to have None)

4 Tap on the **Theme** button to select an effect for when photos move from one to another. If you are showing the photos by connecting the iPad to a TV or AV projector, use the Dissolve transition

5 Tap **On** the **Repeat** option to play the slideshow more than once

6 Tap on the **Play** button to play the slideshow, or the **Pause** button to pause it

Slideshows can also be created from specifically selected photos. Select the photos as shown on page 99, tap on the **Share** button and tap on the **Slideshow** option from the menu.

Emailing Your Photos

You can email your photos to family, friends or work colleagues, directly from the Photos app. To do this:

1 Open the **Photos** app and locate the photo you wish to email using the relevant button at the bottom of the Photos app window

2 Open a photo at full size, or tap on **Select** and tap on a photo to select it

3 Tap the **Share** icon and choose **Mail**

4 Mail will open with the photo already added to the message

If you are emailing very large photos (in terms of file size), check with the recipient first to ensure that their email client can accept large files.

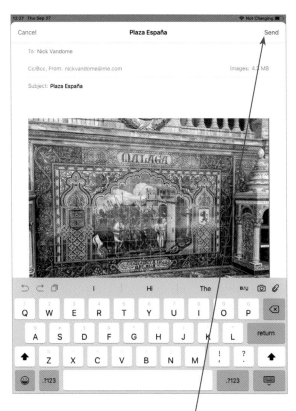

5 Compose the email and tap **Send**

...cont'd

Copying and pasting a photo into an email

1 Select a photo in **Photos**, then tap on the **Share** button and select **Copy**; or press on a photo on a web page and select **Copy**

2 Open **Mail** and select **New Message**

3 Press and hold inside the email body

4 Select **Paste** to paste the image into the email

Emailing multiple photos

1 Open a photo album

2 Tap **Select**

3 Select photos to email (up to five at a time)

4 Tap **Share** (top left) and choose **Mail**

5 The photos will be inserted into a blank email

Hot tip

You can paste photos into an email. You can even paste multiple photos into the same email.

Hot tip

iOS 12 makes it incredibly easy to share your pictures with Facebook, Twitter, etc. Tap the **Share** icon and choose the relevant social network. If you have not added an account you'll be prompted to do so.

Adding Photos to Contacts

It's easy and more personal to assign a photograph to your contacts than leaving them blank.

1 Open **Contacts**

2 Find the contact to which you want to add a photo

3 Tap **add photo** next to the person's name

4 Tap **Choose Photo**

5 You will be presented with your photo albums and imported photos

6 Select the photo you want to use

7 Move and scale until you're happy with the size and position

8 Tap **Choose**

Alternative method

1 Find a photo in the **Photos** app and tap on it to open it

2 Tap the **Share** icon

3 Choose **Assign to Contact**

4 Choose the contact you want, and voilà – the photo will be placed into the photo box for your contact

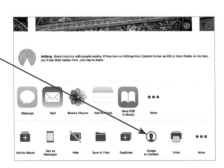

Hot tip

Personalize your contacts by adding photographs.

Use Photos as Wallpaper

Wallpaper, as well as being something you paste onto the walls of your house, is also the term for the backdrop used for the iPad screens. Apple has produced some gorgeous wallpapers for you to use, but you can use your own images if you prefer.

1 Find the photo you want to use in **Photos**

2 Tap to open the picture at full size

3 Tap the **Share** icon

4 Tap **Use as Wallpaper**

You can use your own photos as wallpapers, as well as images saved from the web and email.

5 You will then have the option to use this for the **Lock Screen** or **Home Screen**, or both

TV App

Movies and TV shows can be watched on your iPad, using the TV app. To do this:

1 Tap on the **TV** app

2 Tap on the **Store** button

3 Swipe up and down, and left and right, to view the available content in the TV Store, which links to content in the iTunes Store

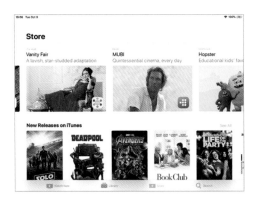

4 Tap on an item to view its details. Tap on these buttons to buy or rent an item

5 Swipe down the page in Step 3 and tap on these buttons to access the linked content in the iTunes Store

The TV app is an updated version of what was previously the Videos app.

Don't forget

Tap on the Search button on the bottom toolbar in Step 3 to access the Search box for looking for specific items and trending items in the TV Store.

Hot tip

Use an HDMI/Lightning Connector cable to connect your iPad to a High Definition TV, and watch content from the TV Store on a TV.

...cont'd

Controls

When watching TV shows or movies on the TV app, or video content such as that on YouTube, the controls are fairly standard. They can also be used in conjunction with an Apple headset, if this is being used to view video content on an iPad. The main controls and actions to note include:

Drag the volume slider in the bottom left-hand corner to change the volume.

Tap the screen twice when a movie is playing to make it fill the screen. Tap twice again to make it fit the screen.

Picture in Picture is a feature on the iPad with iOS 12 whereby video content plays in a separate, minimized window, so that other tasks can be performed while the video plays.

Pause video	Tap here to pause	
Resume playing	Tap here or press center button on Apple headset	
Increase/decrease volume	Drag volume slider control (see tip) or use buttons on Apple headset	
Start item over	Tap and drag the playhead all the way to the left or tap here	
Skip to next chapter (if item contains chapters)	Tap here or press the center button twice on Apple headset	
Skip to previous chapter (if item contains chapters)	Tap here or press the center button three times on Apple headset	
Fast forward/Rewind	Touch and hold these buttons	
Move to specific point in item	Drag the playhead at the top of the screen	
Scale item to fill screen	Tap here to fill screen	
Scale item to fit screen	Tap here to fit the screen	
Minimize the screen to a Picture in Picture	Press the **Home** button	
Stop watching movie before the end	Tap **Done** to quit the TV app	

7 Keeping up with Events

With your iPad in hand, you can always keep up-to-date with the latest news and events. The News app can be used to view news stories from a variety of selected sources, and with the Podcast app you can listen to a range of audio and video broadcasts covering topics from current affairs to comedy.

The layout of the News app has been updated in iOS 12.

Hot tip

Below the **Following** heading in Step 3 is a **Suggested By Siri** heading that contains topics based on Siri searches. Tap on the heart icon to add a topic to your news feed.

Getting the News

The News app is a news aggregation app that collates news stories from a variety of publications, covering a range of categories. To use the News app:

1 Tap on the **News** app

2 Tap on the **Today** button to view the current news stories

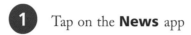

3 The current news stories, based on your news feed, are displayed in the main window

4 Tap on the **Edit** button to the right of the **Today** button

5 Your current news feed items can be removed by tapping on the red circle next to them. The order of importance can be rearranged by dragging these buttons.
Tap on the **Done** button when you're finished

6 Scroll to the bottom of the left-hand panel, as displayed in Step 3, and tap on the **Discover Channels & Topics** button

PERSONALIZE YOUR NEWS
Follow your favorite channels and topics to improve your reading experience.

Discover Channels & Topics

7 Suggested channels and topics are displayed. These can be added to your news feed by tapping once on the heart icon next to an item.
Tap on the **Done** button

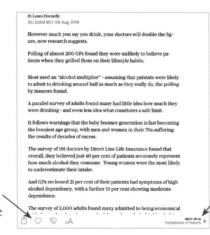

Follow Your Favorites

TOPIC CELEBRITIES
TOPIC POLITICS
TOPIC BREXIT
BuzzFeed
INDEPENDENT
TOPIC TRAVEL
The Telegraph
TIME
CNN
sky news

Done

Don't forget

Scroll down the **Follow Your Favorites** page to view more topics.

8 Tap on a news item in Step 3 to view it in detail

9 When an item has been opened for reading, tap on these buttons on the bottom toolbar to, from left to right: share the item (or save it); follow a news topic for more similar items; unfollow a news topic so you see fewer items; or change the font size

By Laura Donnelly
06:32AM BST 09 Aug 2018

However much you say you drink, your doctors will double the figure, new research suggests.

Polling of almost 200 GPs found they were unlikely to believe patients when they grilled them on their lifestyle habits.

Most used an "alcohol multiplier" - assuming that patients were likely to admit to drinking around half as much as they really do, the polling by insurers found.

A parallel survey of adults found many had little idea how much they were drinking - and even less idea what consitutes a safe limit.

It follows warnings that the baby boomer generation is fast becoming the booziest age group, with men and women in their 70s suffering the results of decades of excess.

The survey of 191 doctors by Direct Line Life Insurance found that overall, they believed just 40 per cent of patients accurately represent how much alcohol they consume. Young women were the most likely to underestimate their intake.

And GPs reckoned 21 per cent of their patients had symptoms of high alcohol dependency, with a further 19 per cent showing moderate dependence.

The survey of 2,000 adults found many admitted to being economical

NEXT UP IN
TRENDING STORIES

Hot tip

Tap under the **Next Up In** option in Step 9 to view the next story for that category; e.g. **Trending Stories** or **Top Stories**.

...cont'd

Under the Spotlight

In the News app it is possible to read more in-depth articles, rather than just the main news headlines. This is done with the Spotlight feature. To use this:

1 Tap on the **Spotlight** button in the left-hand panel

2 The top Spotlight story is featured at the top of the page. Tap on it to read the story

Hot tip

The subjects in the Spotlight section are based on your Channels & Topics selections that were made on page 109.

3 Swipe down the page to view other Spotlight content from different news providers

4 Photo stories are also available in the Spotlight section. Tap on one to view the photos, which are displayed at full-screen size

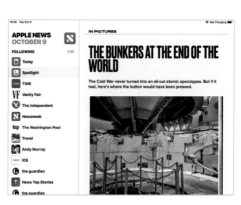

Finding Podcasts

Podcasts are audio or video broadcasts that can be created by individuals or taken from programs that have been broadcast, usually on the radio. In iOS 12, the Podcasts app is one of the pre-installed ones, and can be used to download podcasts. You can search for podcasts from within the Podcasts app:

1 Tap on the **Browse** button on the bottom toolbar to view the currently-promoted podcasts

2 Swipe up and down the screen to view the range of Featured podcasts

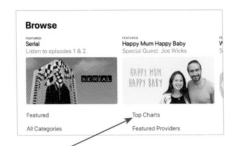

Tap on the **All Categories** button in the Browse section to search for podcasts according to specific topics such as Comedy, News & Politics, Music, or Sports & Recreation.

All Categories

3 Tap on the **Top Charts** button to view the top-ranking podcasts

4 Tap on a podcast to view its details

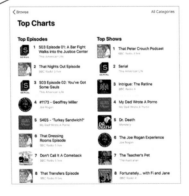

5 Tap on the **Subscribe** button to subscribe to the podcast and download this episode and subsequent ones

Playing Podcasts

Podcasts to which you have subscribed can be played from within the Podcasts app:

1 Tap on the Podcasts app and tap on the **Library** button to view podcasts to which you have subscribed

2 Tap on a podcast to start playing it

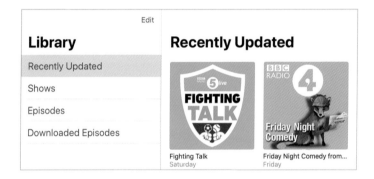

3 Use these buttons on the bottom toolbar to move through the podcast in 15- or 30-second intervals or pause and play it

4 Tap on the **Episodes** button to view all of the episodes of podcast to which you are subscribed

5 Tap on this button next to a podcast to download it to your iPad, rather than playing it by streaming it over Wi-Fi

8 Calendar

You can never be too organized! Calendar makes it easy to set up all of your appointments and add new events as you wish.

Calendar Navigation

The Calendar app has a clear layout and interface, making it easy to enter and edit appointments. The app is designed to resemble a physical calendar, with a left and right page. Each shows different items depending on which view you are using.

In the **Day** view, the left column shows that day's appointments, with any scheduled events spread out on the right. The **Week** view shows the whole seven days with all appointments clearly labeled. The **Month** view shows the whole month's appointments, and the **Year** view shows all of the months for a specific year. The example below is Day view.

View by Day, Week, Month or Year   Search Add Event

Tap to go to Today   View available Calendars   View Invitations

The Calendar Views

You can look at your Calendar using **Day**, **Week**, **Month**, or **Year** views.

Week view showing detailed information for each day

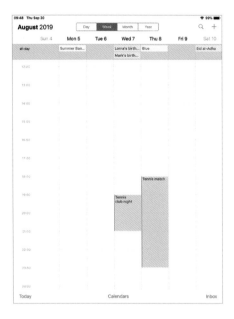

Month view

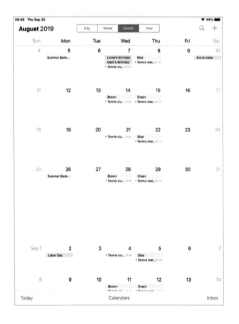

Hot tip

In Month view, you can scroll continuously through the calendar. This means that you do not have to just view a single month on its own; you can view the end of one month and the beginning of the next month in the same calendar window.

Adding Events

You can add events (e.g. appointments) to Calendar directly on the iPad. If the calendar is turned On for iCloud, everything within the app will be available via iCloud and any compatible iCloud devices that also have the Calendar app.

To add appointments directly onto the iPad

116

1 Open the **Calendar** app

2 Tap **+** at the top right of the Calendar window or press and hold on a specific date

3 Enter a title for the event in the **Title** field

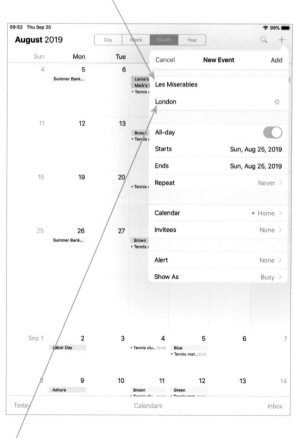

4 Enter a location if necessary in the **Location** field

5 Drag the **All-day** button to **Off**. Tap **Starts** and rotate dials to the required start time

6 Tap **Ends** to add the end time for the event (one hour is the default amount of time, although it can be changed by a minute at a time). Rotate the dials in the same way as for the start time

7 Tap **Repeat** if you want to repeat the event; e.g. anniversary, birthday

8 If you want a reminder tap **Alert** (see image in Step 3)

9 Tap **Calendar** to assign the event to a specific calendar if you have more than one (see image in Step 3)

Don't forget

Alerts can be added for different time periods, and the selection varies depending on how far in the future the event is scheduled for.

Editing Calendar Events

This is very straightforward. Again, you can edit directly on the iPad using any of the views (Day, Week, Month or Year). Tapping the appointment once in Day, Week or Month view takes you straight into Edit mode.

1 Tap the event to open it

2 Tap **Edit**

3 Amend the event, making your changes

4 Tap **Done**

All elements of a calendar event can be edited, including changing it to an all-day event or changing the title and location.

118

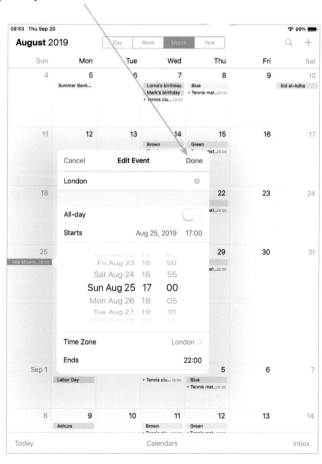

Deleting Events

You can delete appointments in the Calendar app on the iPad. To do this:

1 Tap **Calendar** and open the event by tapping it once. Tap on **Delete Event**, or

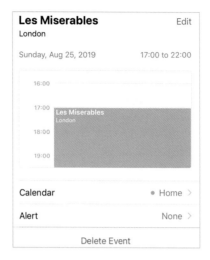

2 Tap on **Edit** in the window above

3 This window is used to edit the items in the event. However, if you then decide to delete the event it can also be done from here

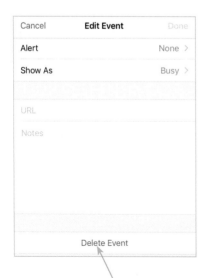

4 Swipe to the bottom of the window and tap **Delete Event** to delete the event

If the Calendar is turned **On** for iCloud, any items that are deleted will also be deleted from any other of your iCloud-enabled Apple devices.

Calendar Alarms

How can you be sure you don't miss a crucial appointment? You could look at the Calendar app daily or more often, and scan through all of the upcoming events.

But an easier way is to set an alarm or a reminder if the event is really important. For example, you might want a reminder two days before an assignment has to be handed in.

On the iPad Calendar, reminders appear as notifications (with sound) on the screen. Set these up by going to **Edit** mode then tap **Alert**. Decide how far ahead you want the alert.

Calendar notifications have to be turned On in order for them to be displayed at the time of the alert. To do this, go to **Settings** > **Notifications**, tap on **Calendar** under the **Notification Style** heading, and drag the **Allow Notifications** button to On.

The alert shows as a notification on the screen (locked or unlocked) at the allocated time, and there will be an alarm sound so you cannot ignore the alert.

9 Contacts

Gone are the days when we just stored contacts on a cell phone SIM card. The world of contacts has become much more advanced, and the Contacts app makes it easy to add and view contacts, making all their details instantly available on your iPad.

Exploring the Contacts App

The Contacts app is a simple but elegant app for managing all of your contact information. The app is designed to resemble a physical address book, showing your **Contacts** and **Groups** down the left-hand page with the selected contact's details shown on the right-facing page.

Groups button   Search box   Add a new contact   Edit contact

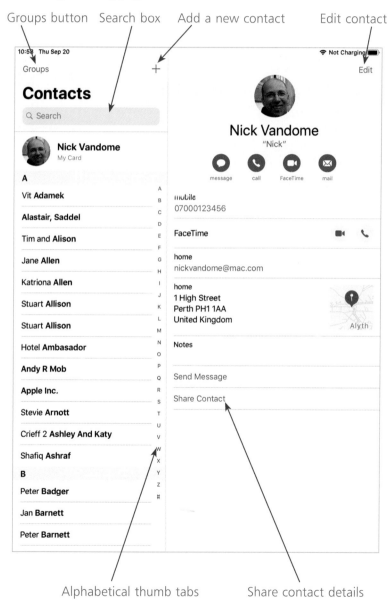

The Contacts app is another one that can be set up for iCloud, so that your contacts are stored here and are available from the online iCloud website, and any other iCloud-enabled Apple devices you have.

Alphabetical thumb tabs   Share contact details

...cont'd

You can also browse Contacts in landscape view but the details are much the same as portrait, although the pages are a bit wider.

Tap on a contact in the left-hand panel to view their details in the right-hand panel.

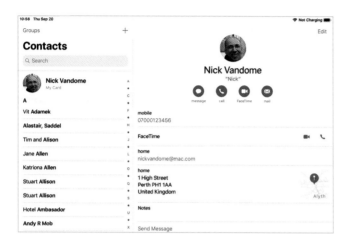

Toggle between Groups and All Contacts

If you have groups, you can access these from within Contacts. Although you can add to a group, you cannot set up a group in Contacts – the group itself needs to be created using your Mac computer Contacts app. To view your groups:

1 Tap the **Groups** button to view all groups

2 Tap a group name to select it and tap on the **Done** button to view the members in the group

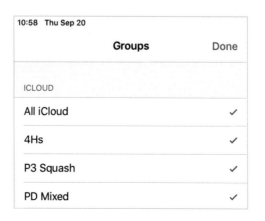

Beware

You cannot create new groups in the Contacts app on the iPad; you can only add to existing ones.

123

Adding Contacts

You can add contacts directly onto the iPad.

To add a new contact:

1 Open **Contacts**

2 Tap the **+** icon at the top of the left-hand page

3 Enter details into the **New Contact** page, adding a photo if you wish

4 Click **Done** when finished

Hot tip

Tap on the green **+** button next to a field to access additional options for it.

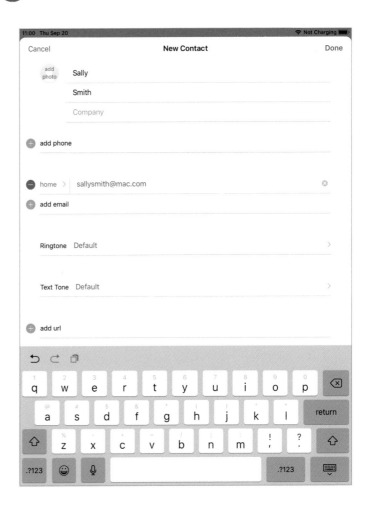

Adding to Groups

With the Contacts app you can also view groups of people for areas such as hobbies, family or work. To do this:

1 Open **Contacts** and tap the **Groups** button to view all groups

2 Tap a group name to select it

3 Tap **Done** to view the contents of the group

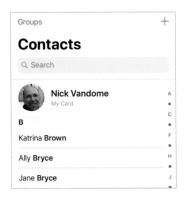

4 Tap the **+** button to create a new entry for the group

5 Enter the details for the new entry (the entry will be added to the group and also All Contacts in the Contacts app). Tap **Done**

On the iPad, Groups in the Contacts app can be used to send a group email to the members of the group.

6 Tap the **Groups** button and tap on **All iCloud** to view everyone in your contacts. Tap **Done** to view your contacts

Edit and Delete Contacts

Edit a contact

This can be done directly on the iPad.

1 Open the **Contacts** app

2 Select the contact and tap on **Edit**

3 Amend the details

4 Tap **Done** when finished

Individual entries for a contact can be deleted by tapping on the red "–" symbol next to them and tapping on the **Delete** button.

Delete a contact

You can delete contacts straight from your iPad. If you have iCloud set up for Contacts, then the contact will be deleted from all iCloud-enabled devices.

1 Open the **Contacts** app

2 Select the contact you want to delete

3 Tap **Edit**

4 Scroll to the bottom of the contact page

5 Tap **Delete Contact**

Assigning Photos

You won't want to have photos for all your contacts, but for family and friends it is great to have their picture displayed in the contacts list.

1 Open **Contacts**

2 Find the contact to which you want to assign a photo

3 Tap **Edit** and tap on **add photo** next to their name

4 Tap **Choose Photo**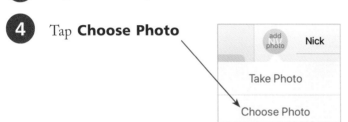

5 Select a photo from those stored on your iPad

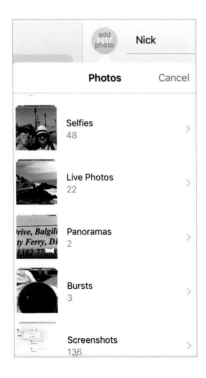

Add photos to friends and family contacts – it makes it more personal.

Hot tip

Sharing Contact Details

You can send a contact's details to a friend using email.

1 Open the **Contacts** app

2 Select the contact you want to share

3 Tap **Share Contact** underneath their details and select an option for sharing, such as **Message** or **Mail**

Send an iMessage to a contact

iMessage is available on iPhone and iPad, and macOS for Mac. Using your iPad you can send an iMessage if you are connected to the internet.

1 Open the **Messages** app

2 Tap the **+** button in the **To:** box to add a contact

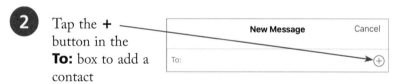

3 Tap on a contact to select them for the message

4 Type your text and tap on the **Send** button to send the message

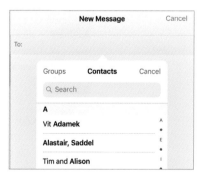

10 Notes

Notes on the iPad takes the place of using pieces of paper to make notes and lists. The app is simple but effective. Not only can you make and store notes on your iPad; you can also add a range of formatting options and store them in iCloud, so you need never forget anything again.

What is the Notes App?

Notes is one of the simplest and most effective of the pre-installed apps. Like several other Apple apps it also operates with iCloud. It resembles a simple, blank notepad. What you see depends on whether you hold the iPad in the portrait or landscape position.

In portrait mode (right) you can see the selected note in a floating window. The landscape mode (below) is more impressive, with a list of notes in the left-hand panel and the current note being viewed on the right.

Each time a note is edited it goes back to the top of the list in the left-hand panel.

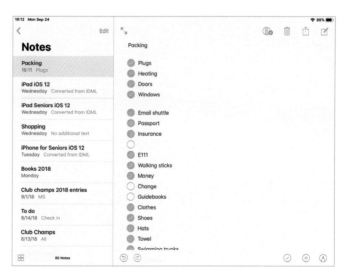

Syncing notes

Notes can be created and stored solely on your iPad, or they can be stored in the iCloud so that they are not only backed up, but also available on other devices.

Adding a New Note

When a new note is created it appears at the top of the list of notes, in the left-hand panel, as shown in the bottom image on the previous page. To create a new note:

1 Tap this symbol at the upper right of the screen

2 A new note is generated

3 Type in your text (since the first line is used as the title of the note, enter something that tells you what the note is about on the first line)

4 To finish, tap **Notes** (upper-left corner of the window) to take you back to the list of notes

If notes are enabled for iCloud (**Settings** > **Apple ID** > **iCloud** > **Notes** > **On**) then all new notes will be saved in the iCloud and available on any other of your iCloud-enabled Apple devices.

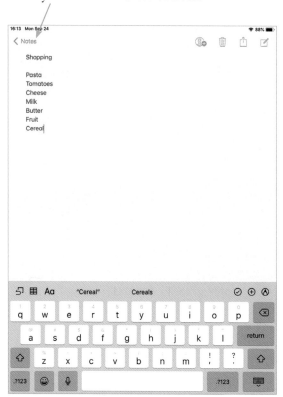

5 Your new note will now be in the list with the date on which it was created or updated underneath it

Formatting Notes

Text in the Notes app can be formatted in a range of different ways, such as adding bold or italics or creating numbered and bulleted lists. To apply formatting to a note:

1 Press and hold at the beginning or end of the piece of text you want to format. Tap on the **Select** button

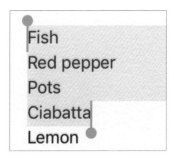

Hot tip

Tap this button once on the Shortcuts bar to cut any selected text.

2 Drag the yellow handles over the text you want to select

3 Tap on this button to access the formatting options

4 Tap on one of the formatting options, such as the Title, Heading or Body options for formatting the font and size, or the list options for creating a list from the selection

5 The formatting is applied to the selected text (in this instance, a numbered list)

6 Tap on this button to create a checklist from the selected text

7 Radio buttons are added to the list (these are the round buttons to the left-hand side of the text)

8 Tap on the radio buttons to show that an item or a task has been completed

9 Tap on this button to take a photo or a video to add to the note (or select the **Photo Library** button to choose an existing photo)

Scan Documents

Take Photo or Video

Photo Library

Add Sketch

Tap on the **Add Sketch** button in Step 9 to add a freehand sketch to a note by drawing on the iPad's screen.

Sharing Items to Notes

In iOS 12, content can now be shared to Notes from apps such as Safari, Maps and Photos. This creates a note with a link to the appropriate app. To do this:

1 Tap on the **Share** button in an appropriate app

2 Tap on the **Add to Notes** button

3 Select whether to create a new note, or add the item to an existing note (**Choose Note:**) and tap on the **Save** button

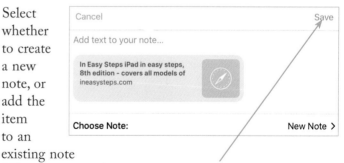

4 The item is added as a note in the Notes app

(11) Maps

Maps makes it easy to identify your location, find places, gauge traffic conditions, and get directions to anywhere or from anywhere – on foot, by car, and using apps for public transport.

What is Maps?

If you have an iPhone you will be familiar with Maps, since the iPad version is pretty similar, although much enhanced. The app shows you a map of where you are, the direction you are facing, street names, directions to a given place from where you are currently (walking, by car and by public transport), and traffic.

The Map app on the iPad shows several views:

- Standard

- Satellite

- 2D or 3D

To use Maps to its full potential you will need an active internet connection – either Wi-Fi or cellular.

To ensure that the Maps app works most effectively, it has to be enabled in Location Services so that it can use your current location (**Settings** > **Privacy** > **Location Services** > **Maps** and select **While Using the App** under **Allow Location Access**).

Transit view can also be used with some locations to display public transport options. However, this is not available for all locations.

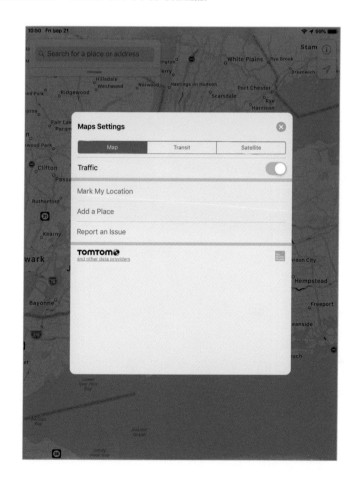

The Maps Views

There are three views, each showing slightly different detail. Standard is probably the most useful, since it shows the typical style of map layout.

Standard view – stylistic but very functional.

Satellite view – as the name suggests, this is a satellite image of the area.

Satellite 3D view – showing parks, water and other terrain.

Use two fingers to move around a map, or rotate it.

Don't forget

The different views can be accessed by tapping on the **i** symbol in the top right-hand corner of the screen.

Hot tip

Tap on the **3D** button in Satellite view to access Satellite 3D view.

Hot tip

Although less glitzy, the Standard view is the most practical in a lot of cases.

Finding Places

You can find a location using a number of methods:

- Address
- By intersection
- Area
- Landmark
- Bookmark
- Contact
- ZIP/postal code

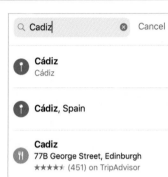

Maps has the ability to show you places of interest.

To find a location

1 Tap the **Search box** to show the keyboard

2 Enter the address or other search information

3 Tap on one of the search results

4 Maps displays the selected item

Zoom in and out

Zoom in	Pinch map with thumb and forefinger and spread apart, or double-tap with one finger to zoom in.
Zoom out	Pinch map with thumb and forefinger and bring together, or tap with two fingers to zoom out.
Pan and scroll	Drag the map up, down, left or right.

Your Current Location

To find your current location

1 Tap on this button

2 A compass will show the direction you are facing

3 Your **location** is shown as a blue marker

The digital compass

 Compass icon – the compass is white, which means it is not active

 Tap the Compass icon and it turns blue and shows North

 Tap again and this icon points to show you the direction you are facing, relative to the map

Hot tip

Tap the compass to find out which direction you are facing. This may save you having to do a U-turn!

Want to know more about your current location?

1 Tap on the blue **location marker** button

2 Details of your location will be displayed

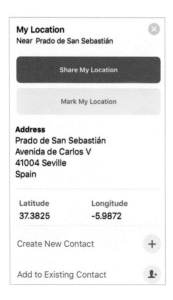

Marking Locations

How to mark locations

You can drop pins onto the map for future reference:

1 Press and hold any location to drop a pin

2 Press and hold to drop another pin at a different location

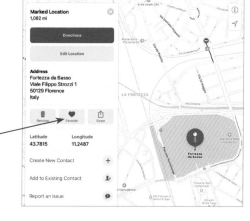

3 To save it, tap the **Favorite** button

Hot tip

To clear a pinned item, swipe from right to left on it in Step 7 and tap on the **Remove** button.

4 In the **Add to Favorites** box, enter a name for the location and tap on the **Save** button

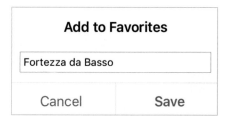

5 The button displays **Favorited**

6 That pin will serve as a marker for future use

7 To see your dropped pin locations, tap in the Search box. A list of your dropped pins will appear. Tap the one you want to view

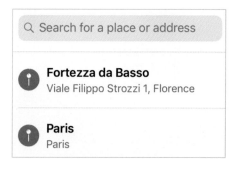

Using Flyover Tour

One of the innovative features in the Maps app is the Flyover Tour function. This is an animated Flyover Tour of certain locations that gives you a 3D tour of a city in Satellite view. To view a Flyover Tour:

1 If the Flyover function is available for the location you are viewing, there will be a **Flyover** option

Beware

The Flyover Tour function is only available for certain cities around the world, with the majority being in the USA. More are being added.

2 Tap on the **Start City Tour** button to start the Flyover Tour (from any map view)

3 The tour starts and takes you through an aerial 3D tour of the main sights of the location

141

Don't forget

When viewing maps, the Compass icon in the top right-hand corner indicates the direction of North.

4 The tour will end automatically, or you can tap on the **Pause Tour** button at any time to pause it. Tap on the cross in the top right-hand corner to stop it at any time

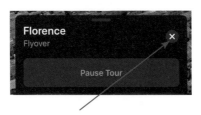

Get Directions

Directions are available for driving, public transport, and walking:

1 Search for a location as shown on page 138

2 Tap on the **Directions** button

Loch Ness
130 mi

Directions
2h 52m drive

3 Select the required mode of transport

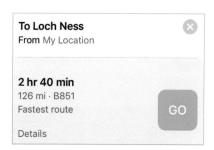

Drive   Walk   Transit

4 Select a route and tap on the **Go** button

To Loch Ness
From My Location

2 hr 40 min
126 mi · B851
Fastest route

GO

Details

Hot tip

For some locations (such as New York and London) there are also transit options when you search for directions within the city location.

5 You can view the directions as an overview or a stepwise guide, by tapping at the bottom of the window and tapping on the **Details** button

Alternatively, you can find directions by using a pin dropped on the map in your desired destination:

1 Tap a **pin** on the map

2 Tap **Directions**

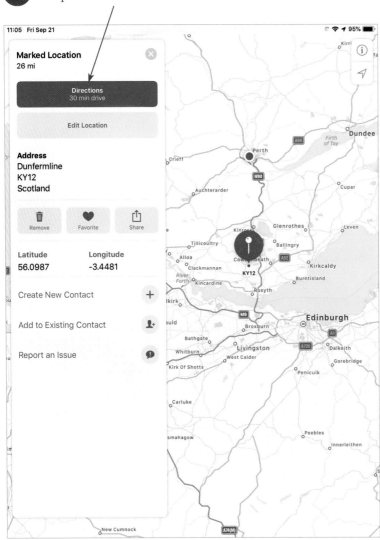

Traffic Conditions

Maps can also show you the traffic conditions for locations. (This feature did not work for all countries or cities at the time of printing.)

1 Tap the **i** symbol in the top right-hand corner of the screen to view the map options, and drag the **Traffic** button **On**

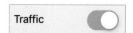

The Traffic option is available in the Standard map view and the Satellite view, but not the Transit view.

2 The traffic conditions are shown as colors:

Green	average speed is >50mph
Yellow	25-50mph
Red	<25mph
Gray	traffic information is not available

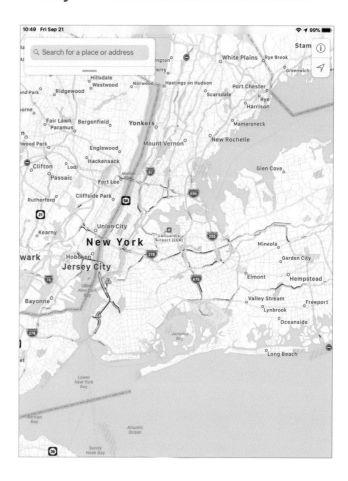

12 Music

The iPad's Music app is a great music player, and now also links to Apple Music, a subscription service that provides access to the entire iTunes library of music.

Starting with Apple Music

Apple Music is a service that makes the entire Apple iTunes library of music available to users. It is a subscription service, but there is a three-month free trial available. Music can be streamed over the internet or downloaded so you can listen to it when you are offline. To start with Apple Music:

1 Tap on the **Music** app

2 Tap on the **For You** button

3 Tap on the **Choose Your Plan** button

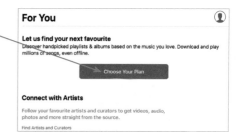

4 Select either an **Individual**, **Family** or a **University Student** membership plan (this will only start to be charged after the free trial ends)

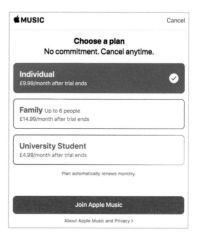

5 Enter your **Apple ID password** (an Apple ID is required in order to use Apple Music), then tap on the **Continue** button

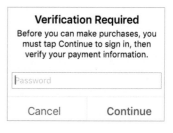

Hot tip

To end your Apple Music subscription at any point (and to ensure you do not subscribe at the end of the free trial), open the **Settings** app. Tap on the **iTunes Stores & App Store** option and tap on your own **Apple ID** link (in blue). Tap on the **View Apple ID** button and under **Subscriptions**, tap on the **Manage** button. Drag the **Automatic Renewal** button to **Off**. You can then manually renew your Apple Music membership, if required, by selecting one of the **Renewal Options**.

iTunes Store

This is covered in more detail in Chapter 14.

In the iTunes Store you can browse categories of available content, which includes:

- Music.
- Films/Movies.
- TV Programs/TV Shows.
- Top Charts.
- Genius.
- Purchased (items you have purchased previously).

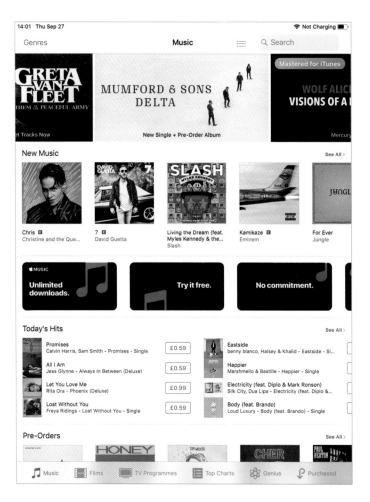

Hot tip

Use the Search box at the top of the iTunes Store window to look for specific items (in any of the iTunes categories).

Buying Music

Music on the iPad can be downloaded and played using the iTunes and the Music apps respectively. iTunes links to the iTunes Store, from where music and other content can be bought and downloaded to your iPad. To do this:

1 Tap on the **iTunes Store** app

2 Tap on the **Music** button on the iTunes toolbar at the bottom of the window

3 Tap on an item to view it. Tap here to buy an album or tap on the button next to a song to buy that individual item

Beware

You need to have an Apple ID with credit or debit card details added to be able to buy music from the iTunes Store.

4 Purchased items are included in the Music app's Library, under the **Recently Added** heading

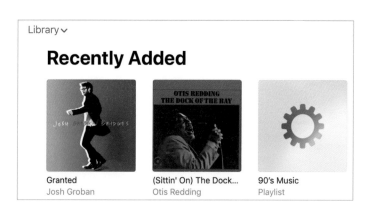

Playing Music

Once music has been bought on iTunes it can be played on your iPad using the Music app. To do this:

1 Tap on the **Music** app

2 Tap on the **Library** button on the bottom toolbar

3 Select an item from the **Recently Added** section, or swipe up the page to view more items

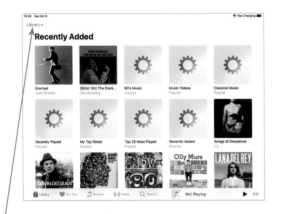

Hot tip

To create a Playlist of songs, tap on the **Playlist** button in Step 4, then tap on the **New** button. Give it a name and then add songs from your Library.

4 Tap on the **Library** button in the top left-hand corner to select different categories for viewing the items in the Music app. Tap on a category to view it

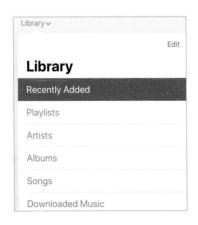

...cont'd

5 Select an item and tap on a track to select it and start it playing

6 Tap here to select menu options for the track, including removing it, adding it to a playlist, playing the next available track, saving the track to play later, or sharing the item via mail, messaging or social media options

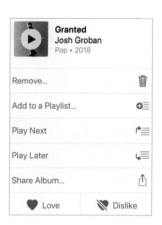

150

7 When a track is playing, tap on the bottom of the Music app to access music controls

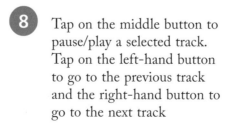

8 Tap on the middle button to pause/play a selected track. Tap on the left-hand button to go to the previous track and the right-hand button to go to the next track

13 The iTunes Store

The iTunes Store is a huge resource for music, movies, TV shows, audiobooks, and other media. The iPad version is simple to use, so you can browse the iTunes Store and download content quickly and easily.

Welcome to the iTunes Store

This app is a great hub for browsing new music, and renting or buying music and other media including:

- Songs and albums

- Videos

- TV shows and movies

- Audiobooks

There are more than 35-40 million music tracks (depending on location) and thousands of movies available for download. Purchases can be made using your Apple ID or by redeeming an iTunes gift card.

You will need an Apple ID to buy things from the iTunes Store (but not view them) and for many functions on the iPad. If you haven't got one, it would be best to set one up.

First, log in to your iTunes account with your Apple ID

1 Tap **Settings**

2 Tap **iTunes & App Store**

3 Tap **Sign In**

4 Enter your Apple ID **username** and **password**

If you don't have an iTunes account with an Apple ID

1 Tap **Settings**

2 Tap **iTunes & App Store**

3 Tap **Create New Account**

4 Follow the instructions to lead you through the setup process

The iTunes Store has >35 million music tracks, >1 million podcasts, and >65,000 movies.

You can also create an Apple ID directly from the Apple website at https://appleid.apple.com/account

Layout of the iTunes Store

Swipe left and right on the top panels to view the items. Swipe up and down to see the rest of the options on the page.

Finding content using Genres

Tap on the **Genres** button in the top left-hand corner to view the available genres for a category.

Hot tip

An extensive range of educational material can also be accessed from the iTunes U app, which can be downloaded from the App Store.

Music

Browse music by tapping the **Music** button at the bottom of the iTunes Store screen.

You can browse a range of **Genres**, including:

- All Genres

- Alternative

- Blues

- Classical

- Dance

- Pop

Genius is a great way of finding new music.

Tap on the **Genius** button at the bottom of the screen to view recommendations based on previous purchases.

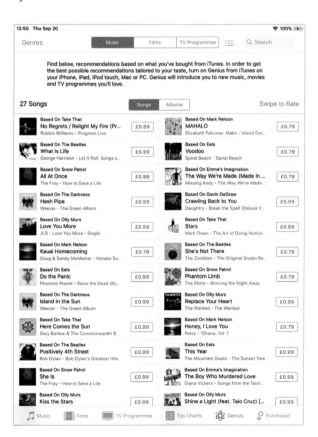

Movies

The Store makes it easy to browse for movies and to rent or buy these. You can browse by Genres including: Action & Adventure, Classics, Comedy, Kids & Family, Romance and Thriller.

Previewing movie information

1. Tap on an item to open an information window that shows the cost of rental or purchase

2. Select the required format; e.g. HD (High Definition) or 4K video

3. Under the **Trailers** heading, tap on the thumbnail to see a short preview of the film before you buy

4. Tap the price to **Buy** or **Rent**, and the movie will download to your iPad

5. Tap the **Share** icon to send a link to the movie by email or message, or upload to Twitter or Facebook (if set up). You can also **Gift** the movie to a friend

Once you have downloaded an item to rent, you have 30 days to start watching it, and 48 hours to complete viewing it once you have started.

TV Shows

Just like Movies, you can buy or rent TV Shows directly from the iTunes Store.

You can browse a range of **Genres**, including:

- All Genres

- Animation

- Comedy

- Drama

- Kids

- Non-Fiction

Don't forget

Movies and TV shows take up more storage space on your iPad than content such as music or books.

Just follow the same process as for Movies, described on page 155.

Audiobooks

As the name suggests, audiobooks are books that are listened to rather than read. These are ideal if you have visual problems, or if you find it easier to listen to a book; for instance, if you're exercising or driving.

There are many titles available in the iTunes Store, but there are many other sites listing free and paid audiobooks for downloading to your iPad:

- **http://www.audible.com (or .co.uk)**

- **http://www.audiobooks.org**

- **http://librivox.org**

Hot tip

Enter **audiobooks** or **audio books** in the iTunes Search box at the top of the window to view the options.

Genius Suggestions

If you are stuck for ideas for what to buy in terms of music, films, or TV shows you can let Genius make suggestions for you. Genius will look at your previous purchases and make suggestions for you. If you have never bought a TV show using iTunes Store it will say *"You do not currently have any recommendations in this category"*.

To see the Genius suggestions, tap the Genius button at the bottom of the iTunes Store page and select a category at the top.

Above you can see items that Genius has suggested I might buy, based on previous purchases.

14 The App Store

The App Store is a vast repository of apps for the iPhone and iPad. The number of third-party apps grows by the day. You can browse and purchase from this burgeoning store right from your iPad, and increase its capabilities with additional functionality.

App Store Layout

The App Store is Apple's online store, where users of iOS devices can review and download apps for almost any activity imaginable. Some apps are free, whilst others have to be paid for.

At the time of printing, over 1 billion iOS devices have been sold and there are over 2.1 million apps in the App Store, of which at least 1 million are native to the iPad. Overall, there have been more than 180 billion downloads (all iOS apps).

The layout of the App Store has been updated in iOS 12.

Hot tip

With so many apps available, it is difficult to find new apps easily. Use the **Search** option on the bottom toolbar of the App Store to look for specific apps.

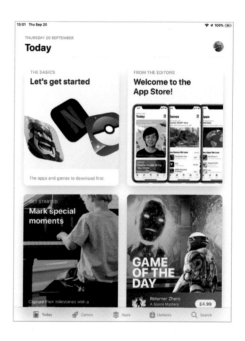

Hot tip

Even if you delete a previously-purchased app from your iPad, you can download it again for free by tapping the **Updates** tab at the bottom of the App Store screen, from where you will be able to access your purchased apps. Apple will not charge you again for the app.

To view the options in the App Store:

● Tap **Today** on the bottom toolbar to view the currently-featured items.

● Tap **Games** on the bottom toolbar to see the latest games.

● Tap **Apps** on the bottom toolbar to see the latest apps.

● Tap **Updates** on the bottom toolbar to update your apps, if updates are available.

What are the most popular apps?

Some of the popular app categories are: Books, Games, Entertainment, Education, and Utilities.

Featured Apps

The **Apps** section displays new and recommended apps. This changes frequently, so there will be a lot of new apps appearing here on a regular basis. Swipe up and down to view the available content in the Featured section.

Within the **Apps** section are various categories that can help you further refine your app search. These change on a regular basis, depending on the range of apps that are selected to be featured. Tap on the **See All** link to the right-hand side of each category to see more. Some of the most regular categories that can be found on the Apps homepage are:

New Apps We Love
This shows the apps deemed to be the best new ones in the Store.

Popular Apps To Try
Some of the apps that are being downloaded the most at any given time.

Top Paid
The top-selling, paid-for apps.

Top Free
The most downloaded free apps.

Don't forget

If there is a major global event taking place, such as the Olympic Games, there may be an app section on the Featured page with apps relative to this event.

161

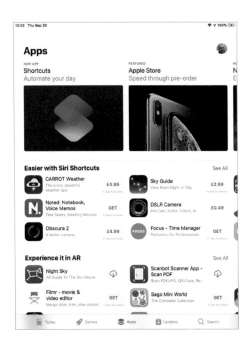

Top Charts

These apps are the most popular. The screen below shows the **Top Paid** apps in the top panel, and the **Free** apps below them. These are displayed on the main Apps page, below the featured items.

Beware

Do not limit yourself to just viewing the top apps. Although these are the most popular, there are also many more excellent apps within each individual category.

Hot tip

Use the **Search** box on the bottom toolbar to look for specific apps. When search results are displayed after looking for a specific app, there is an option to view **iPad Only** apps or **iPhone Only** apps (select **Filters** > **Supports** and then the required item). Sometimes an app may be designed specifically for the iPhone, but this can still be downloaded to the iPad.

Tap on the **See All** button to view all of the Top Paid apps and the Top Free apps.

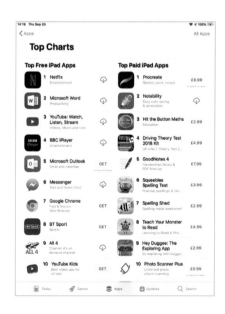

Categories

There are currently 24 categories of apps in the App Store. This helps (slightly) to find what you're looking for, but with more than 1 million apps, finding an app can be quite difficult! For example, if you tap Lifestyle, you will see more than 2,000 apps.

Searching Categories

1 Swipe down the Apps homepage and tap on the **See All** button to view all of the available categories

Top Categories   See All

⚙ AR Apps   🗑 Entertainment

● Kids   ✏ Productivity

🎵 Music   📷 Photo & Video

2 Swipe down to see the full list of categories

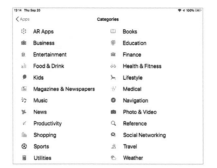

3 Tap on a category to view the items within it

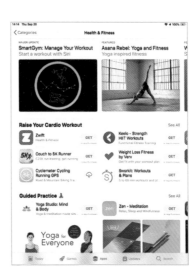

Buying Apps

When you identify an app that you would like to use, it can be downloaded to your iPad. To do this:

1 Find the app you want to download, and tap on the button next to the app (this will say **Get** or will have a price)

2 Tap on the **Install** button

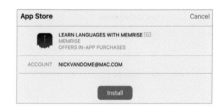

Apps usually download in a few minutes or less, depending on the speed of your Wi-Fi or cellular connection.

3 Enter your Apple ID details and tap on the **Sign In** button

Some apps have "in-app purchases". This is additional content that has to be paid for when it is downloaded.

4 The app will begin to download onto your iPad

5 Once the app is downloaded, an icon is added to your Home screen. Tap on it to open and use the app

Keeping Apps Up-To-Date

App publishers regularly update their software, ironing out bugs and making improvements. The App Store makes it very easy to see if there are any updates for the apps you have downloaded.

How to determine whether updates are available

- You should see a red badge at the top right of the App Store icon. The number in the circle tells you how many updates you have waiting to be downloaded.

- If you don't see a badge, there may still be updates available. Open the **App Store** app, tap **Updates** and if there are any, these will be listed. If none are available then you will see **Updated Recently** apps.

- You can update one at a time or all at once.

- The app updates will download in the background.

Apps can be set to install updates automatically, from within **Settings** > **iTunes & App Store**, by dragging the **Updates** button to **On** under **Automatic Downloads**.

165

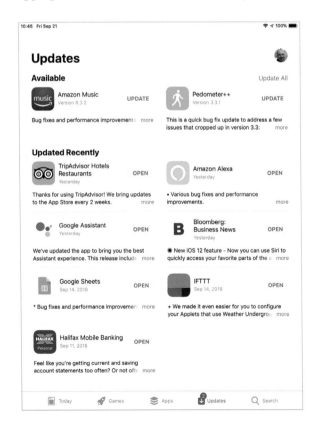

Submitting Reviews

Reviews are quite useful since they may help you decide whether to buy an app or not.

You can submit reviews for any apps you have downloaded (free or paid).

You cannot review any app you do not own.

When you are viewing apps you can read their reviews by tapping on the **Reviews** tab, next to the description of the app.

You have to download an app before you can review it.

Even if an app is total rubbish you cannot give it zero stars!

166

1 Tap the **App Store** icon to launch the app

2 Find the app you want to review

3 Under **Ratings & Reviews** you should see **Tap to Rate**

4 Tap on the stars to rate the app between one and five stars (you cannot give any app a zero-star rating)

5 Tap on the **Write a Review** button

6 Enter your text

7 Tap **Send**

8 You can amend the star rating before you hit the Send button

Deleting Apps

There are several ways you can remove apps from the iPad:

- Directly using the iPad itself.
- Choosing *not* to sync an app using iTunes on your computer.

Deleting directly from the iPad

1 Press and hold an app's icon until all the icons start jiggling

2 Tap the **X** on the top-left corner of the app

3 A box will pop up warning you that you are about to delete an app and all of its data

4 If you still want to delete the app press **Delete**

5 Press the Home button again to stop the apps jiggling

Deleting from within iTunes

1 Connect the iPad to your computer

2 Open **iTunes** > **Apps**

3 You will see your iPad screen shown in the right panel of the iTunes Apps pane

4 Find the app you want to delete and hover your pointer over it until an **X** appears at the top left of the app's icon

5 Click the **X** to delete the app

The app will then be removed from your iTunes and also from your connected iPad.

Although the app has gone from the iPad, you can still re-download it from the App Store if you wish, or you can resync the app back to the iPad later from your computer if you have backed it up there.

Some of the pre-installed apps (see page 26) cannot be deleted.

If you delete an app on the iPad you can re-download it from the App Store again if you wish. You won't be charged for it again.

iTunes U

Although not strictly part of the
App Store, the iTunes U app can be
downloaded from here and used as a
great educational resource. iTunes U
is a distribution system for lectures, language lessons, films,
audiobooks, and lots of other educational content.

iTunes U
Free educational courses
★★★☆☆ 188

Finding educational material on iTunes U

Universities & Colleges	Search for content by educational institution (not every university is listed at present).
Beyond Campus	Other agencies offering educational material for download.
K–12	Content for Primary and Secondary education.

Using iTunes U

Finding content in iTunes U is very similar to using the App
Store: iTunes U has a **Features** and **Top Charts** section, as
well as a comprehensive search facility. Tap on the **Get** button
when you find a suitable course.

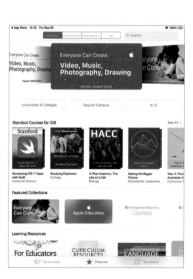

Organizing Apps

When you start downloading apps you will probably soon find that you have dozens, if not hundreds of them. You can move between screens to view all of your apps by swiping left or right with one finger.

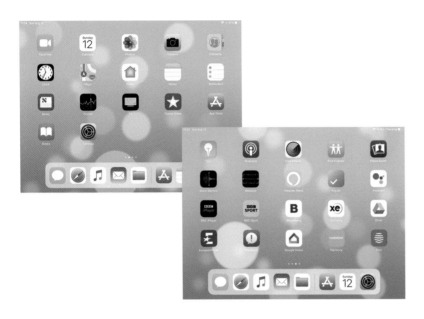

Hot tip

To move an app between screens, tap and hold on it until it starts to jiggle and a cross appears in the corner. Then, drag it to the side of the screen. If there is space on the next screen the app will be moved there.

As more apps are added it can become hard to find the apps you want, particularly if you have to swipe between several screens. However, it is possible to organize apps into individual folders to make using them more manageable. To do this:

1 Tap and hold on an app until it starts to jiggle and a cross appears at the top-left corner

Don't forget

When new apps are downloaded, the new icon will be automatically placed at the end of the last screen.

2 Drag the app over another one

...cont'd

3 A folder is created, containing the two apps

4 The folder is given a default name, usually based on the category of the apps

5 Tap on the folder name and type a new name if required

6 Click the Home button once to finish creating the folder

7 Click the Home button again to return to the Home screen (this is done whenever you want to return to the Home screen from an apps folder)

8 The folder is added on the Home screen. Tap on this to access the items within it

Beware

Only top-level folders can be created; i.e. sub-folders cannot be created. Also, one folder cannot be placed within another.

Hot tip

If you want to rename an app folder after it has been created, tap and hold on it until it starts to jiggle. Then tap on it once and edit the folder name, as in Step 5.

Hot tip

For the latest range of iPad Pros that do not have a Home button, swipe up from the bottom of the screen to return to the Home screen after creating a new folder.

(15) Books

Books is an elegant app that lets you browse the Book Store and save books and PDFs on your bookshelf for reading later. You can read, highlight, use the dictionary, change the appearance of the books, and much more.

The Books App Interface

The iPad is ideal for reading electronic documents including ebooks and PDFs, and this is a key feature for many people buying the iPad. Just as Apple has made it simple to buy music and other digital content for the iPad, it has done the same with electronic books – ebooks. Browsing and purchasing is simple, and previewing books before you buy is also possible, saving you from buying books you don't want.

The **Books** app provides you with an online **Store** and also a **Library** section to store books you have purchased or loaded yourself.

The layout of the Books app has been updated in iOS 12.

A PDF is a document created in the Portable Document Format. This is a versatile format that can be opened and read on a variety of devices. You need to have some form of Adobe Acrobat Reader (or equivalent) functionality on your device to read PDFs.

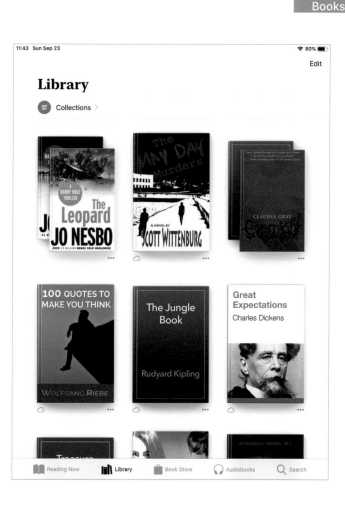

The Library bookshelf

- You can rearrange the books in the Library by tapping **Edit** in the top right-hand corner and then tapping on books to select them.

- **Move** a book to your chosen position by holding on it and dragging it to a new position.

- **Delete** books by tapping on the **Trash** button and tapping on **Remove Download**.

Left: You can browse your collections to see Books, PDFs, etc. Click on the Edit button as above to manage individual titles.

Bottom left: Select a book by tapping on it and tap on the **Share** button to share it a variety of ways.

Below right: Tap on the **Add to...** button and select a location to add the book to (it will still be available in the Library).

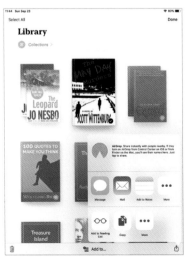

Open a Book

Books (ebooks and PDFs) are stored on shelves in your Library. Just like a real library, you can browse your collection, open and read books, add bookmarks, and more.

1 Tap **Books**

2 Tap **Library** if Books opens on the Store page

3 Select a book to read – tap to open

4 Choose a specific point to start reading, by sliding your finger along the slider at the bottom

If you close the app or book, Books will remember the place, and the next time you open it the book will be opened at the same page as you left it.

Hot tip

See page 188 for details on purchasing ebooks from other sources.

Flicking through a book

1 Tap **Books** to open the app, and choose a book to read

2 Move through the pages by **tapping the right or left margins** (moves you forward and backwards through the book). Or, you can **touch and hold the bottom corner** moving your finger towards the top left

3 Alternatively, to move to the previous page, touch and hold the left margin and slide your finger left to right across the screen

To move to a specific page in a book

1 Tap the page in the center. Controls will appear on the screen

2 Drag the slider at the bottom of the screen to the page you want

Viewing the Table of Contents

1 Tap the page in the center. Page controls should appear

2 Tap on the **Contents** button

Add as many bookmarks as you want to your book – and remove them just as easily!

Add a bookmark

This helps you find your place in a book (you can add multiple bookmarks).

1 While the book is open, touch the bookmark icon to add a new bookmark (it will turn red)

Great Expectations AA Q

Chapter VIII

2 Remove the bookmark later by tapping on the red bookmark icon

...cont'd

Want the book read to you?

You will need to activate VoiceOver
(**Settings** > **Accessibility** > **VoiceOver** – see page 231).

Highlighting text

You can use highlighters on a physical book to mark specific pieces of text, and the same can be done using an ebook:

Hot tip

Using VoiceOver (see page 231), the iPad can read books to you (not PDFs, though).

1 Open the page of a book

2 Press and hold your finger on a word within the text that you want to highlight

3 Drag the blue anchor points over any text that you want to select

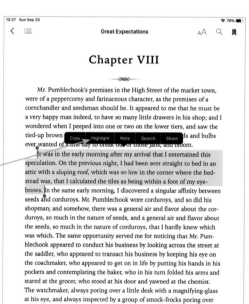

4 Choose **Highlight** from the pop-up menu. Select a color with which you want to highlight the text

5 To remove the highlights, press on the text again to select it, tap on the Highlight option, and tap on the Trash button

Using the Dictionary

The in-built dictionary is instantly accessible when reading your ebooks, but not within PDF files:

1   Open the page of a book and tap and hold the word you want to look up in the dictionary

2   Tap **Look Up** from the pop-up menu

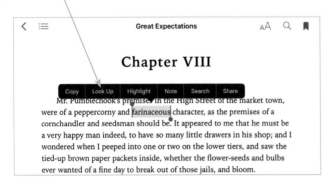

The dictionary is not available when reading a PDF.

3   The phonetic pronunciation and definitions will appear in a pop-up box

4   Tap on the **Done** button to close the dictionary

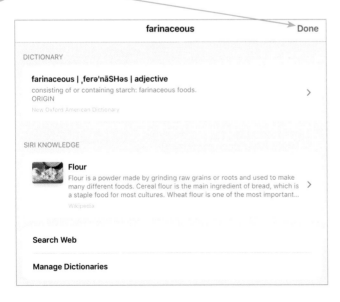

Find Occurrences of Words

You can search an entire book or document for the occurrence of a specific word:

1 Open the page of a book

2 Tap and hold the word for which you want to find occurrences

3 Tap **Search**   Search

A drop-down list of all pages containing that word will appear.

In the search results, tap on an occurrence of a word to view it in context in the book.

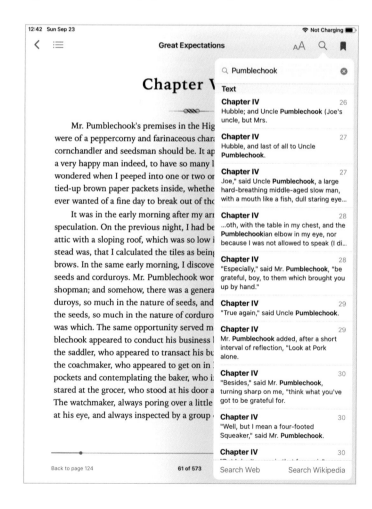

Adjust the Screen Brightness

Depending on the ambient lighting, you may need to adjust the screen brightness. For example, if you read in a dark room you could turn the brightness down, whereas outside in sunshine you might need to turn the brightness up. To adjust the screen brightness:

1 With the page of a book open, tap on this button on the top toolbar

2 Tap and drag the slider left and right to adjust the brightness

Beware

If the screen brightness is too high, it could cause headaches when reading for a long time.

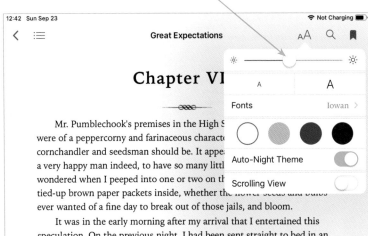

Portrait or Landscape?

The iPad adjusts the orientation of the page depending on how you hold it. If you turn it sideways, the pages rotate. This is not particularly convenient when you are lying down.

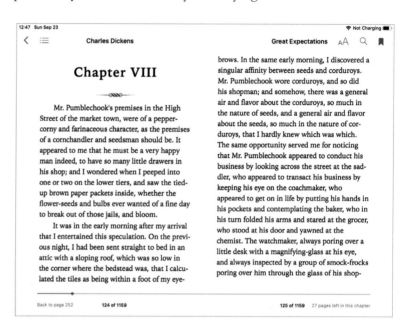

To avoid automatic rotation of the book pages:

1 Open a book

2 Hold the iPad in either portrait or landscape mode

3 Swipe down from the top right-hand corner of the screen to access the Control Center

4 Tap on this button so the screen rotation is locked, indicated by the icon turning red

Hot tip

Reading a book is one of the occasions when it is definitely useful to lock the screen, especially if you are lying down!

Using the Book Store

This is a great resource, containing many of the popular titles, with more being added daily. The Book Store is like iTunes except you buy books rather than music, and there is no rental option. Browsing the Book Store requires an active internet connection.

The top featured books are displayed at the top of the window. Scroll down the window to view more featured categories, such as **For You**, **New & Trending**, **Books We Love**, **Top Charts** and **More to Explore**.

Beware

You need an Apple ID even if you want to download free books.

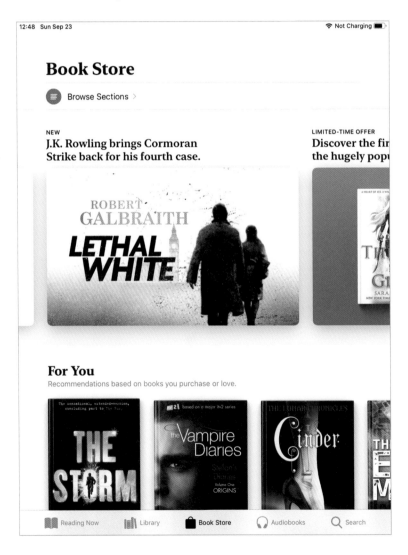

...cont'd

Browsing is made incredibly easy. You can browse by category or search for specific items, using the **Browse Sections** button.

You can search books by some of the following categories:

- **New & Trending**
- **Top Charts**
- **Books We Love**
- **Special Offers & Free**
- **Award Winners**
- **Bestsellers**
- **Rave Reviews**
- **Genres**

...cont'd

Sample chapters

You can't download music samples in iTunes, although you can hear 30-second audio samples before you buy. However, you *are* allowed to download short sample chapters of books before you commit to buying them. If you like the sample you will probably go back and buy the full title.

Downloading sample chapters

1 Open **Books** and find a book that you are interested in

2 Tap the book cover to bring up the information window that floats on top of the current page

3 Tap the **Sample** button and this will be downloaded to your library. This will usually be one or two chapters of the title

Sample chapters are available for most books so you can try before you buy.

183

4 Tap the sample in your Books Library to open it and start reading

Changing Fonts and Size

Sometimes the font or font size can make it difficult to read a book. With a physical book you cannot change the font, but with ebooks you can control the typeface and its size, to make the book as readable as possible.

To change the font or font size:

1 Open a book in Books

2 Decide which orientation you will use to read the book – portrait or landscape

3 Tap on this button AᴀA

4 Tap the small or large **A** to make the font smaller or larger

5 To change the font itself, tap **Fonts**

6 Choose from the drop-down list

184

7 Tap here to select a background color for the book's pages; e.g. white, sepia, gray or black

Purchasing Books

Providing you have an Apple ID, you can download paid or free books from the Book Store.

1 Open **Books**

2 Tap **Store** if you are currently in Library mode

3 Find a book you want to buy

4 Tap its icon to bring up the floating window showing the price

5 Tap **Buy** (if the book is free, it will say **Get Book** instead)

If you have the Books app on other Apple devices such as an iPhone or a MacBook, then you will be able to read any books you have bought here too.

Photoshop Elements 2018
Tips, Tricks & Shortcuts in easy steps
Covers versions for both PC and Mac users
Nick Vandome >

BUY | £8.99

+ WANT TO READ   SAMPLE

Publisher Description

Photoshop Elements is well established as the premier consumer photo-editing software, and the latest release is Photoshop Elements 2018. This enhances the software's reputation as a powerful and easy-to-use option for photo-editing, with a range of features for editing and creating photo effects and also a powerful Organizer for managing your photos.... **More**

GENRE	RELEASED	LENGTH	PUBLISHER	LANGUAGE	SIZE
Computing & Internet	**2018** 15 February	**192** Pages	In Easy Steps Limited	**EN** English	**22.8** MB

Tap on the **Sample** button in Step 5 to download a free sample of the book.

6 The book will begin to download into your library and the view will change from Store → Library. You will be prompted for your **Apple ID password**

7 Once entered, the book will download

Find More Books by Author

If you have a favorite author, or you just want to find more books by the same author, you can:

1 Tap the book cover in the Store to bring up the information screen with a range of details about the book

2 Scroll down the page

3 You will then see any other books available on the Book Store by the same author

Setting up Books alerts based on items that you have previously downloaded can be done in the Settings app: go to **Settings** > **iTunes & App Store**, tap **Apple ID**, then tap **View Apple ID**. Sign in with your password and scroll down to **My Alerts** > **Manage**. Drag the **Email alerts based on downloads** to **On** to receive alerts based on items that have been downloaded from iTunes, including books, music, movies, etc.

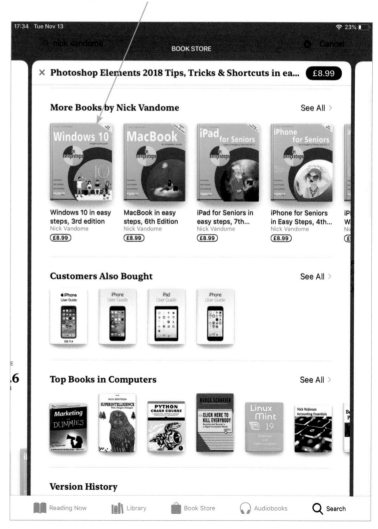

Tell a Friend

You can let other people know about books by sending links to books that they can view on their computer:

1 In the Book Store, tap on a book title to view its details and tap on this button

2 Tap **Share Book**

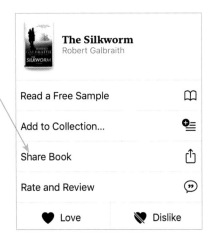

3 Select one of the sharing options including messaging, emailing, or sharing via a social networking site, if any of these have been set up on your iPad

4 Depending on the selection in Step 3, a link is included to the selected item, so that the recipient can then view it in the Book Store

If you see something great, share it with a friend. It's very easy to do.

Tap on this button to the left of the button in Step 1 to send a book as an electronic gift to someone.

Ebooks from Other Sources

You are not completely limited to the Book Store for your electronic books for the iPad:

Epub books

1 Download an epub book (**epubbooks.com**) on your PC or Mac

2 Add to iTunes (drag and drop the book straight onto iTunes)

3 Connect the iPad, then sync epub books to iPad

Other sources for ebooks

● Smashwords (**smashwords.com**).

● Google Books (**books.google.com**). The homepage for this is the Google Search box, which searches over the Google library of books rather than a standard Google search.

Search the world's most comprehensive index of full-text books.

My library

● Kindle iPad app (**amazon.com**).

● Design your own – many programs allow you to export your files in epub format; e.g. Adobe InDesign, Storyist, Sigil Ebook, and others. Whatever software you use, if it can be saved in the epub format, you can get it onto the iPad. Another option is to save your work as a PDF, but remember: you cannot search PDFs for words, or use the dictionary. It does let you read the document easily, though.

Don't forget

The Book Store is not the only source of ebooks for the iPad. Most books in epub format will work with the iPad.

(16) Smart Homes

Smart homes that contain devices that can be controlled by apps and digital voice assistants are now becoming more widespread, as the technology becomes more user-friendly and affordable. On the iPad, smart home devices such as smart lighting and smart heating can be controlled using the Home app and Siri.

About Smart Homes

The concept of the smart home – i.e. one in which electronic devices are controlled via apps on a mobile device (such as an iPad), voice controls, or accessed remotely – is not a science-fiction vision of the future; it is very much part of the here and now, and a realistic and affordable option. For a smart home to work to its full potential there are a number of elements that can be in place:

- Smart home devices.

- Apps on smartphones and tablets, such as the Home app on the iPad, and online access.

- Digital voice assistants, or hubs.

Range of devices

Also known as the Internet of Things (IoT), smart home technology now spans a wide range of devices (and this is increasing regularly) as manufacturers realize the commercial importance of smart homes. Some of the current devices are:

Hot tip

An iPad can be used to set up Apple's HomePod smart speaker, using the Home app. It can also be used to set up an Amazon Echo smart speaker and a Google Assistant smart speaker. This is done by downloading the Amazon Alexa app and the Google Assistant app respectively from the App Store.

190

Hot tip

Digital voice assistants can be linked to smart home devices so that they can be controlled by voice commands.

- **Smart lighting systems**, including smart light bulbs and a bridge that connects to your Wi-Fi router. Individual lights can be controlled around the home with an app, a digital voice assistant or a remote control. Groups of lights can also be used to create artistic effects. Smart lighting apps contain a range of settings that can be used to give you maximum control and flexibility over your lighting system.

- **Smart thermostats**. Heating systems can be controlled to turn them on and off and set the temperature. Smart thermostats can also be used to determine whether there are people at home, and regulate the temperature accordingly. In this way, they can be used to save money on your heating bills.

- **Smart security systems**. Extensive security systems using external cameras can be installed, controlled and viewed via an app.

- **Smart locks**. In addition to security cameras, smart locks can be used to add additional security to your home. They can be activated by key cards, key fobs, apps, digital voice assistants, time-limited PIN codes, and even remotely.

- **Smart cameras**. Individual cameras can be used within the home, such as for monitoring a baby's bedroom or the outside of a property.

- **Smart plugs and sockets**. Individual smart plugs can be used throughout the home, so that devices can be turned on and off without having to physically press a switch.

- **Robotic lawn mowers and cleaners**. Tasks within or outside the home can be automated through the use of robot lawn mowers, vacuum cleaners and mops. These do not all have their own compatible apps, although some do, but can work independently.

Smart home apps on the iPad

Although it is not essential to use apps with smart home devices, it rather defeats the purpose of them if this valuable option is ignored. Most smart home devices have a companion app that can be used to control the device, either in the home, or remotely. Remote access can require registering with the device's related website; e.g. if you are using the Philips Hue smart lighting system, you can register at the Philips website and then control your lighting system when you are away from home.

Smart home apps offer significant functionality, depending on the type of smart home device, and some of the options include:

- Turning devices on and off.

- Using preset scenes (for devices such as smart lighting) to create a variety of color combinations.

- Setting timers so that devices turn on and off at specific times; e.g. set smart heating to come on in the morning and turn off in the evening, and also a variety of times in between.

- Creating customized routines to give ultimate control over your smart home devices.

Hot tip

Smart home apps can be downloaded to an iPad from the App Store. For instance, download the Philips Hue app to control smart lighting. The iPad Home app can also be linked to smart home devices. Once this is done, Siri can be used to control linked smart home devices.

Using the Home App

On Apple mobile devices using iOS 12, such as the iPad, the Home app can be used to link to smart home devices so that they can be controlled by the app and by Siri. To use the Home app:

1 Tap on the **Home** app on the iPad's homepage

Home

2 Tap on the **Get Started** button to start adding a smart home device

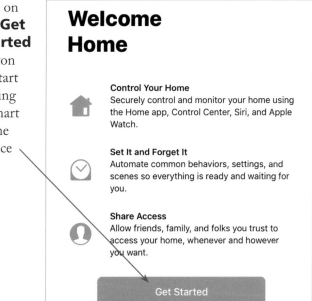

Welcome Home

Control Your Home
Securely control and monitor your home using the Home app, Control Center, Siri, and Apple Watch.

Set It and Forget It
Automate common behaviors, settings, and scenes so everything is ready and waiting for you.

Share Access
Allow friends, family, and folks you trust to access your home, whenever and however you want.

Get Started

3 Tap on the **Add Accessory** button to add a smart home device to the Home app

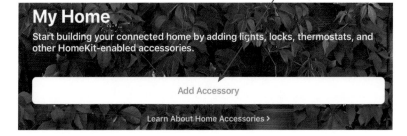

My Home
Start building your connected home by adding lights, locks, thermostats, and other HomeKit-enabled accessories.

Add Accessory

Learn About Home Accessories >

4 The camera on an iPad can be used to identify the code for the device. This is usually an eight-digit code on part of the device; e.g. the hub for a smart lighting system, or the smart thermostat for a smart heating system. Position the camera so that it can see the code, which is done within a white box. The code should then be captured automatically

Hot tip

If there is no code visible, or you cannot scan it with your device's camera, tap on the **Don't Have a Code or Can't Scan?** link in Step 4 and follow the instructions.

5 Tap on the required item that has been identified

...cont'd

6 Details about each item that is connected to the device are displayed

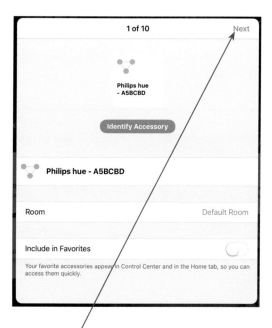

Each smart home device has to be added separately to the Home app before it becomes available for use.

7 Tap on the **Next** button   Next

8 For a device such as a smart lighting system, each light bulb that has been installed is listed. Tap on the **Next** button to move through all of the items

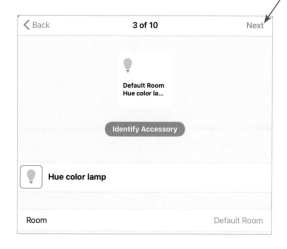

...cont'd

9 The final listing for the device is indicated here

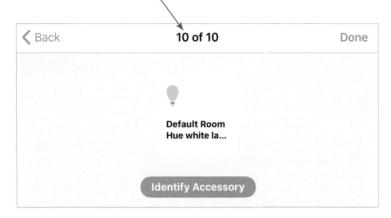

(Within image)

⟨ Back   **10 of 10**   Done

Default Room
Hue white la...

Identify Accessory

10 Tap on the **Done** button   Done

11 All of the items that have been added for a specific device are displayed on the Home app homepage

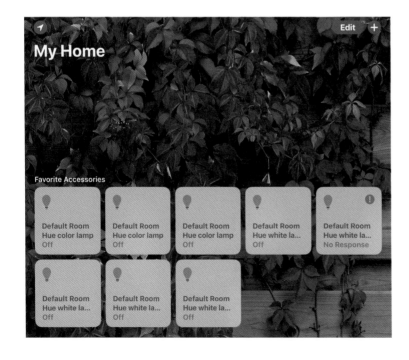

Once items have been added to the Home app they can then be controlled with voice commands on an iPad using Siri. Access Siri and try a command such as, "Siri, turn on living room", to turn on the smart lights in the living room. The action will also be reflected in the Home app.

Managing the Home App

Once devices have been added to the Home app they can be managed within the app. This also enables Siri to control the devices, in response to voice commands. To manage devices:

1 Open the **Home** app and tap on the **Home** button on the bottom toolbar

2 Tap on an item on the homepage to activate it

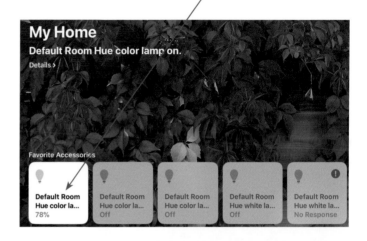

It is important to assign devices to specific rooms, so Siri knows where the items are located and can respond to voice commands accordingly. See pages 200-202 for details.

3 Tap on the **Details** button to view details of the currently-activated item

4 Tap on the **Done** button

...cont'd

Editing the Home app

The appearance of the Home app can be customized, and it is also possible to invite other people to have access to the app so that they can control smart devices with it too. To do this:

1 Tap on the **Edit** button in the top right-hand corner of the homepage

2 Tap the arrow to the right of **My Home**

3 Tap under the **Name** heading to change the name of the homepage

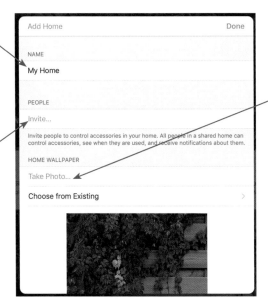

4 Tap on the **Invite...** button to invite someone else to use the Home app

Hot tip

Tap on **Take Photo...** or **Choose from Existing** to select a new background for the Home app.

| HOME WALLPAPER |
| Take Photo... |
| Choose from Existing |

197

5 Enter the email address of the person that you want to invite, and tap on the **Send Invite** button

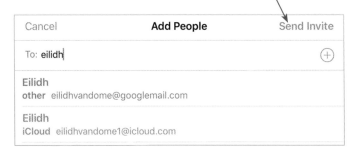

Beware

Scroll down to the bottom of the page in Step 3 and tap on the **Remove Home** button to remove the current home devices. This will remove all of the items that have been added.

Remove Home

Managing Rooms

The Home app can also be used to assign rooms to specific devices. This can be useful if you have several of the same type of device: once rooms have been assigned for devices you can instruct Siri accordingly; e.g. "Hey Siri, turn on the smart plug in the living room", or "Hey Siri, turn on the bedroom lights". To assign rooms to specific smart home devices:

1 Open the **Home** app and tap on the **Rooms** button on the bottom toolbar

2 Tap on the **Edit** button in the top right-hand corner

3 Tap on the right-pointing arrow next to **Default Room**

4 Under the **Room Name** heading, enter a new name for the default room

5 Tap on the **Done** button in the top right-hand corner

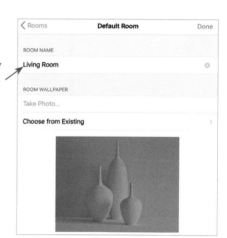

6 The room's new name is shown on the **Rooms** homepage

Beware

Give rooms common, recognizable names so that if other people are accessing the Home app they will be able to find the rooms easily.

Adding rooms

To add more rooms to the Home app:

1 Tap on this button above the current room name

2 Tap on the **Add Room** button

Add Room	Living Room	Done

ROOM NAME

Living Room

Before a new room is added, the current room name is displayed in Step 2.

3 Enter a name for the new room, under the **Room Name** heading, and tap on the **Save** button

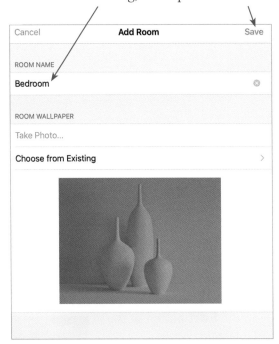

...cont'd

4 Tap on the **Done** button

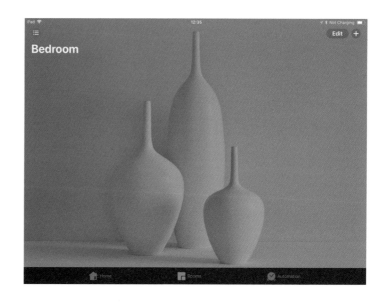

‹ Rooms	**Bedroom**	Done

ROOM NAME

Bedroom

5 The new room is displayed in the Rooms section of the Home app. At this point it is empty; i.e. it does not have any devices assigned to it

Hot tip

Swipe left and right on the Rooms homepage to view the different rooms that have been added.

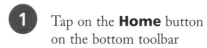

Bedroom

Assigning devices
Once a room has been added, devices can be assigned to it:

1 Tap on the **Home** button on the bottom toolbar

2 Tap on the **Edit** button in the top right-hand corner

...cont'd

3 Tap on one of the devices on the homepage

4 The device's current location is displayed under the **Room** options. Tap on this to edit the room

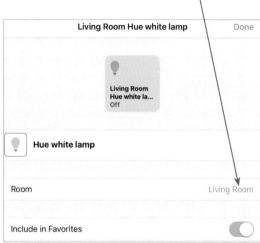

5 Tap on a new room to assign it to the device

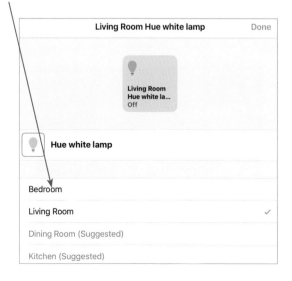

Hot tip

Drag the **Include in Favorites** button **On** in Step 3 to display the device on the homepage of the Home app. Drag it Off to hide it.

Beware

Devices do not have to be physically located in the room specified in the Home app. However, if they are in a different location they will be turned on and off according to their location in the app. Try to ensure that the physical location and the location specified in the app are the same.

...cont'd

6 Tap on the **Done** button to assign the selected device to the room and return to the Home app homepage

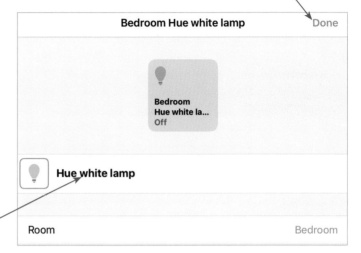

Hot tip

Device names can be edited by tapping on them here and overtyping the current name. This can be useful, as it means they can be given names that are specific to the rooms in which they are located.

7 Tap on the **Done** button in the top right-hand corner of the Home app homepage to finish assigning the device to the selected room

8 Tap on the **Rooms** button on the bottom toolbar to view devices that have been assigned to specific rooms

(17) Productivity

Doing productivity tasks need not always be a chore, and the iPad makes writing documents, number-crunching and giving presentations a pleasure! Instead of dragging a heavy laptop to your next meeting, try taking your iPad instead and use the Pages, Numbers, and Keynote apps for all of your productivity needs. Office and Google productivity apps can also be used on the iPad.

Accessing Productivity Apps

Since productivity is now a genuine option on the iPad, there is a whole category dedicated to it in the App Store. This contains a wide range of productivity apps that can be downloaded and managed in the same way as for any other apps from the App Store. To access the productivity apps:

Don't forget

The App Store bottom toolbar is the same for all categories and consists of **Today**, **Games**, **Apps** and **Updates**.

1 Tap on the **App Store** app

2 Tap on the **Apps** button on the bottom toolbar

3 Swipe down the page and tap on the **See All** button under the **Top Categories** heading

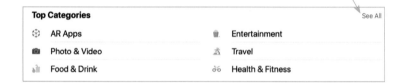

Top Categories   See All

☼ AR Apps   🏛 Entertainment

📷 Photo & Video   ✈ Travel

🍴 Food & Drink   🚲 Health & Fitness

Don't forget

Apps can also be searched for using the Search box, which is accessed from the **Search** button on the bottom toolbar.

4 Tap on the **Productivity** button   ✎ **Productivity**

5 The featured productivity apps are displayed

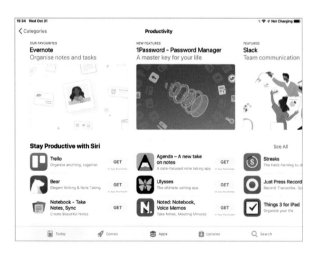

6 Swipe up and down and left and right to view all of the featured apps

iWork Apps

Apple has its own range of productivity apps that can be used for word processing, spreadsheets, and presentations. They are known as the iWork suite of apps and consist of Pages, Numbers, and Keynote. These are free to download from the Productivity category of the App Store. To do this:

1 Tap on the **Search** button on the bottom toolbar and type iWork into the Search box

2 Tap on the **Get** button for each of the apps

3 Each of the apps has templates from which content can be created, and they can also be used with iCloud Drive to save and share files

Using Apple Pages

Pages is Apple's word processing app and it has been developed to a point where it is a realistic option for creating documents in the workplace. The first step in Pages is to create a new document. This can either be a blank template, or one from a template that includes pre-inserted content. To do this:

Pages is not a built-in app, but it can be downloaded for free from the App Store.

1   Tap on the **Pages** app

2   Tap on the **+** button

3   Tap on either one of the blank templates for a file with no content, or one with pre-inserted content

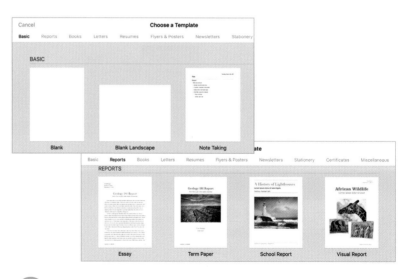

The document is opened with the document type in Step 3 as its default name, displayed at the top of the page.

Visual Report

4   Tap on the file name at the top of the page (see second tip) to select it and overwrite it with your own content

Saving documents

When a document is created in Pages it is automatically saved within the Pages file structure. From here it can be viewed and renamed. To do this:

1 From within the current document you are working on, tap on the **Documents** button

Documents

Once a document has been created and saved within Pages, it is also available within the iCloud Drive app and can be accessed from there on other compatible devices.

2 The new document is displayed within the **Pages Recents** window

Pages Recents

Conservation Report
Today at 15:51
247 KB

3 Tap on the document name to select it and enter a new name for the document

Wildlife Report

4 Tap on the **Done** button

Done

5 Tap on the document, or any other in the **Pages Recents** window, to open it

Pages Recents

Wildlife Report
Today at 15:51
247 KB

...cont'd

Working with text

Once a new document has been created in Pages, content can be added, usually starting with text:

1 Tap on the page and start typing where the cursor appears

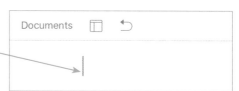

2 Press and hold at the insertion point (where the cursor appears) to access options for selecting text, pasting copied text, highlighting text, or adding a comment

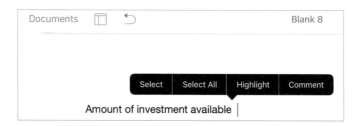

Don't forget

When a word is selected, the blue handles around it can be dragged to select text to the left or right of it.

3 Double-tap on a word to select it and access the text-editing toolbar

Don't forget

The options in Step 3 include: cutting, copying, pasting or deleting the selection; replacing it with another word; looking up a dictionary definition; or copying the text style so that it can be pasted onto another piece of text.

4 Tap on this button on the shortcuts toolbar to select a specific font

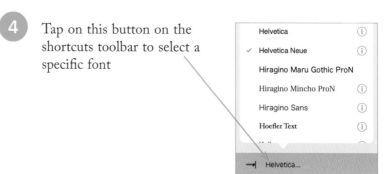

...cont'd

5 Tap on this button at the right-hand side of the shortcuts toolbar to select a font size

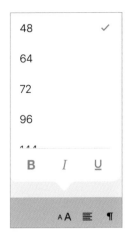

Tap on this button at the far left-hand side of the shortcuts toolbar to access options for selecting the next tab position and indenting or outdenting text.

6 Tap on this button at the right-hand side of the shortcuts toolbar to align text

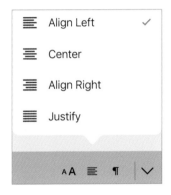

7 Tap on this button at the right-hand side of the shortcuts toolbar to add the required formatting options

Page Breaks, Section Breaks and Column Breaks in Step 7 are non-printing items, which means they will not appear in any printed versions.

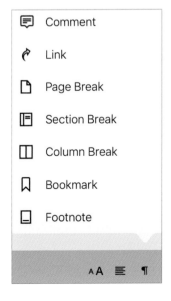

...cont'd

Adding graphics

Pages has considerably more functionality than just displaying text – it can also include a variety of graphical elements:

1 Open a document and tap on this button on the top toolbar

2 Tap on this button to view the options for adding tables

3 Tap on this button to view options for adding charts

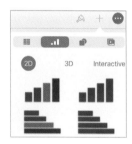

4 Tap on this button to view options for adding objects

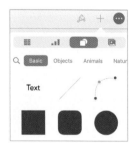

5 Tap on this button to view options for adding photos or videos, either from the Photos app, iCloud Drive, or a new one taken with the iPad's camera

Working with graphical elements

Once graphics have been added in Pages they can have content
added to them and have their format edited. To do this:

1 Tap on an item to select it.
Drag on the resizing handles
to change its size

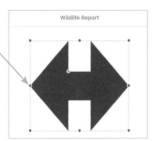

Press and hold on an
object to drag it into a
new position within the
document.

2 For a chart, tap on the chart and tap on the **Edit Data**
button to add your own data for the chart

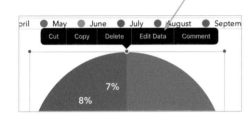

In Step 4, tap on the
Arrange button to
access options for how
text wraps around the
selected object. This can
then be used to format
the text and objects in
your document.

3 Enter data
in the **Edit
Chart Data**
window and tap
on the **Done**
button

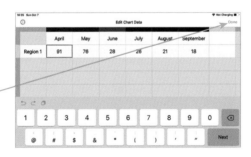

4 Tap on this button
on the top toolbar for
additional formatting
options for the
selected item

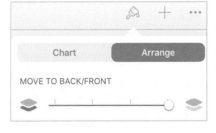

Using Apple Numbers

Numbers is Apple's spreadsheet app that can be used for entering data, creating charts and graphs, and conducting a range of calculations through the inclusion of formulae. To start creating a spreadsheet with Numbers:

1 Tap on the **Numbers** app

2 Tap on the **+** button

3 Tap on either one of the blank templates for a file with no content, or one with pre-inserted content

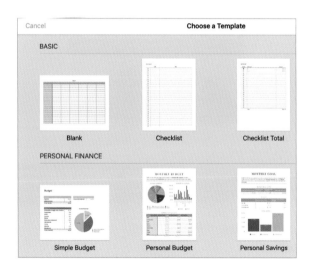

4 For a spreadsheet with pre-inserted content, tap on the content to select it, and overwrite it with your own data

Numbers is not a built-in app, but it can be downloaded for free from the App Store.

Tap on the **Spreadsheets** button at the top left-hand side of the window to access the main Numbers window, if it is not displayed, for creating a new spreadsheet.

Spreadsheets

Saving spreadsheets

When a spreadsheet is created in Numbers it is automatically saved within the Numbers file structure. From here it can be viewed and renamed. To do this:

1 From within the current spreadsheet you are working on, tap on the **Spreadsheets** button

Spreadsheets

The default name for a new spreadsheet is the one used for its original template in Step 3 on the previous page. If more than one spreadsheet is created from the same template without renaming the previous one(s), each new spreadsheet will have the same name but with an incremental number added to the file name for identification; e.g. Simple Budget and Simple Budget 2.

2 The new spreadsheet is displayed within the **Numbers Recents** window

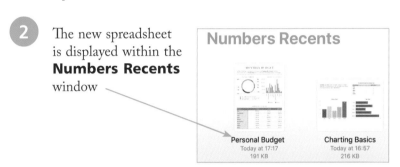

213

3 Tap on the spreadsheet name to select it and access the **Rename Spreadsheet** window

4 Enter a new name for the spreadsheet

5 Tap on the **Done** button

Done

6 Tap on the spreadsheet, or any other in the **Numbers** window, to open it

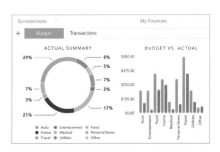

...cont'd

If a new, blank spreadsheet is created, this will consist of one large table. Spreadsheets created using the pre-formatted templates can consist of several tables.

Tap on this button at the end of the columns control bar to add a new column.

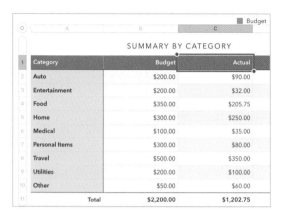

Tap on this button at the bottom of the rows control bar to add a new row.

Selecting items

Content in Numbers is added within tables. This can be one large table for the whole spreadsheet, or several separate tables within a single spreadsheet. Being able to select specific elements within a table is essential to working effectively within Numbers.

1 Tap on a single cell to select it and display the row and column controls

Category	Budget	Actual
Auto	$200.00	$90.00
Entertainment	$200.00	$32.00
Food	$350.00	$205.75
Home	$300.00	$250.00
Medical	$100.00	$35.00
Personal Items	$300.00	$80.00
Travel	$500.00	$350.00
Utilities	$200.00	$100.00
Other	$50.00	$60.00
Total	$2,200.00	$1,202.75

SUMMARY BY CATEGORY

2 Tap on a letter in the top toolbar to select a column and display the relevant toolbar

Category	Budget	Actual	Difference
Auto	$200.00	$90.00	$110.00
Entertainment	$200.00	$32.00	$168.00
Food	$350.00	$205.75	$144.25
Home	$300.00	$250.00	$50.00
Medical	$100.00	$35.00	$65.00
Personal Items	$300.00	$80.00	$220.00
Travel	$500.00	$350.00	$150.00
Utilities	$200.00	$100.00	$100.00
Other	$50.00	$60.00	($10.00)
Total	$2,200.00	$1,202.75	$997.25

3 Tap on a number in the left-hand toolbar to select a row and display the relevant toolbar

Category	Budget	Actual	Difference
Auto			$110.00
Entertainment	$200.00	$32.00	$168.00
Food	$350.00	$205.75	$144.25
Home	$300.00	$250.00	$50.00

SUMMARY BY CATEGORY

4 Press and hold on this button and drag to move the whole table

Beware

When tables are resized, the content does not resize in proportion. Therefore, some of the content in each cell could be obscured if the cells become too small for the content.

215

5 Tap the button in Step 4 and drag the blue resizing handles to resize the whole table

6 Drag here when a row is selected, to resize it

7 Drag here when a column is selected, to resize it

Hot tip

Resize columns and rows to ensure that text can fit in them with enough space around it, particularly for items such as main headings.

...cont'd

Adding data

Data is the lifeblood of a spreadsheet, and different types of data can be entered using Numbers:

1 Double-tap on a cell to access the data-entry keyboard. Use the data-entry keyboard as required; this changes for the different items

2 Tap on this button to enter numerical data

3 Tap on this button to enter date and time

...cont'd

4 Tap on this button to enter text

Don't forget

Numbers can be entered into the data-entry field from the Text button, but if you are entering a lot of figures it is probably quicker to use the Numbers button.

5 Tap on this button to enter a formula for the cell

Don't forget

Tap on these buttons that appear at the left-hand side and the right-hand side of the Formula data-entry field to accept or reject a formula.

6 Tap on this button to add automated actions to a cell; e.g. the current time updates constantly so that it will always show the correct time

217

Using Apple Keynote

Keynote is Apple's presentation app, and it has been developed to a point where it is a realistic option for creating presentations in the workplace. The first step in Keynote is to create a new presentation. This can either be a blank template, or one from a template that includes pre-inserted content. To do this:

1 Tap on the **Keynote** app

2 Tap on the **+** button

3 Tap on one of the templates as the basis for the new presentation

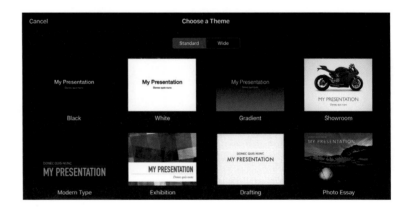

4 Tap on content to select it and overwrite it with your own content

Saving presentations

When a presentation is created in Keynote it is automatically saved within the Keynote file structure. From here it can be viewed and renamed. To do this:

1 From within the current presentation you are working on, tap on the **Presentations** button

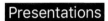

The thumbnail in the Keynote window displays the first slide of a presentation.

2 The new presentation is displayed within the **Keynote Recents** window

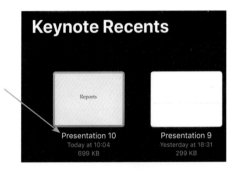

3 Tap on the presentation name to select it and access the **Rename Presentation** window

4 Enter a new name for the presentation

Use presentations sparingly, so that your audience does not become bored with them. They should be one in a range of methods for delivering information, not the only one.

5 Tap on the **Done** button

6 Tap on the presentation, or any other in the **Keynote Recents** window, to open it

...cont'd

Playing presentations

The main purpose of creating a presentation is to be able to play it to an audience. This can be done via a projector onto a screen, or the iPad could be used directly with its larger screen. When playing a presentation there are a number of tools that can be used by the presenter to aid the process. To play a presentation:

1 Tap on the first slide of the presentation in the slides panel

2 Tap on this button on the top toolbar

3 Tap on each slide to move forwards to the next one

Hot tip

To exit Presentation mode before the end of the presentation, pinch inwards with two fingers.

4 Press on a slide to access the presentation tools at the bottom of the screen and buttons for moving forwards or backwards

Don't forget

The presentation starts playing at the slide that is selected in the slides panel in Step 1.

220

Microsoft Office Apps

One of the great advances for productivity on the iPad has been the availability of compatible versions of Microsoft Office apps, including Word, Excel, PowerPoint and OneNote. For many people these are the apps of choice for productivity tasks, as they are frequently used in working environments. These apps can now be downloaded from the App Store, and various subscription models are available to access their full functionality. To start working with Microsoft Office apps:

1 Open the App Store and tap on the Search button on the bottom toolbar. Enter **Office 365**

2 Tap on one of the apps to view its details

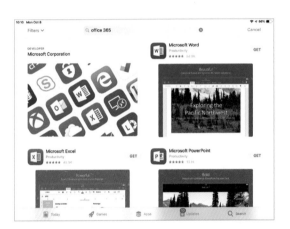

The free versions of the Office apps can only be used to view documents. For the full functionality you need to take out a subscription that is renewed monthly (see pages 222-223).

221

3 Tap on the **Get** button to download the app

GET

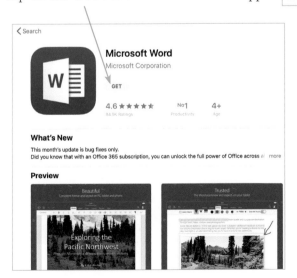

When you create a subscription for one of the Office apps, you automatically get access to the others in the suite: the subscription is for Office 365 rather than a specific app.

Opening Office Apps

The iPad versions of the Office apps – Word, Excel and PowerPoint – are free to download from the App Store, but this only allows you to view documents; you cannot create or edit them. For this necessary functionality you need to create a Microsoft Account and select a subscription model for using the app. To do this:

1 Tap on one of the Office apps to open it

2 Tap on the **Sign in** button if you already have a Microsoft Account. If not, tap on the **Create an Account** button (an account can be created, for free, with an email address and a password)

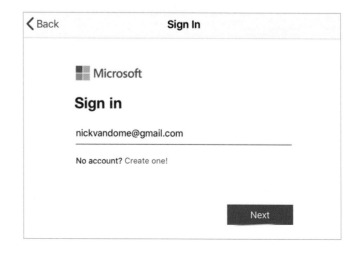

3 Once you have a Microsoft Account, enter your email address and tap on the **Next** button

Don't forget

Documents created in Office apps on an iPad can be stored in OneDrive, Microsoft's online storage and sharing service. Download the OneDrive app from the App Store to use this.

4 Enter your Microsoft Account password and tap on the **Sign in** button

Although the Office apps are Microsoft products, the subscription is paid through your Apple ID account, as the apps are sold through the App Store.

5 By default, you get a free month's trial of the Office apps, which starts once you sign in with your Microsoft Account. Tap on the **Create and Edit** button to start working with the app, or the **Upgrade Now** button to view your subscription details

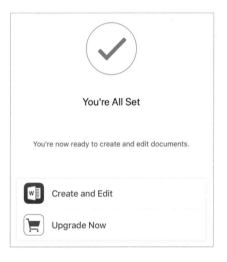

To cancel the Office 365 subscription, tap on the **Settings** app and tap on the **iTunes & App Store** tab. Tap on your **Apple ID** name and tap on **View Apple ID**. Under **Subscriptions**, tap on **Manage**. Tap on the Office app name under **Subscriptions** and drag the **Automatic Renewal** button to **Off**.

6 Tap on one of the subscription models. This takes you to a sign-in for the iTunes Store. Enter your Apple ID password to start the subscription

223

Google Productivity Apps

There is a range of Google productivity apps that are similar to the Apple and Microsoft ones in terms of covering word processing, spreadsheets and presentations. The Google versions are Google Docs, Google Sheets and Google Slides, and they can all be downloaded from the App Store.

Don't forget

The Google Drive app can also be used to store photos and videos.

These are designed to be used within the Cloud, using the Google Drive app. To do use this you must have a Google Account, which can be created when you first open one of the apps by entering an email address and a password. Once this has been done you can starting using the Google productivity apps.

Don't forget

Documents created in the Google productivity apps can be shared between different devices without using Google Drive, but this gives greater flexibility in terms of accessing them through a browser too.

1. Tap on one of apps and tap on the **Sign In** button

2. Enter your Google Account email address and tap on the **Next** button

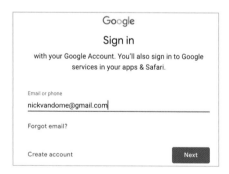

3. Enter your Google Account password and tap on the **Next** button to start using the app

...cont'd

Using Google Drive

While the Google productivity apps can be used on their own, they gain additional flexibility if Google Drive is also used for storing your content. To do this:

1 Access **Google Drive** in the **App Store** and download it

Google Drive – online backup
Cloud storage space
★★★★★ 175K

2 Tap on the **Google Drive** app to open it

3 Tap on the **Sign In** button to sign in with your Google Account details

4 The **My Drive** folder displays any items that you have created with the Google productivity apps. Tap on an item to open it

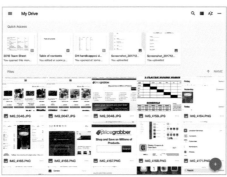

5 Tap on this button to create a new folder; upload items into Google Drive (including from iCloud Drive); take a photo; or create a document with one of the Google productivity apps

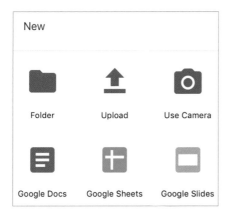

Hot tip

If you are already signed in to one of the Google productivity apps on the previous page, you will not need to enter your sign-in details again when you tap on the Google Drive Sign In button.

Don't forget

If you try to create a new document with one of the Google apps that you have not downloaded onto your iPad, you will be prompted to do so when you tap on the app in Step 5.

Dropbox

Another useful productivity option is the file storage and sharing service Dropbox. This is a Cloud-based service and it is not linked to any specific operating system (e.g. iCloud for Apple, OneDrive for Microsoft, or Google Drive for Google), and so can be used on a variety of devices and operating systems. Dropbox can be used to back up documents and files and also share them with other people. To use Dropbox on the iPad:

1 Open the App Store and download the Dropbox app

2 Tap on the **Dropbox** app to open it, and register with an email address and password

3 Tap on the **Files** button on the bottom toolbar to view items that are in Dropbox

4 Tap on the **Create** button on the bottom toolbar to add a content type to Dropbox. This includes scanning documents; uploading photos from your device; creating or uploading files; and creating folders within the Dropbox file structure

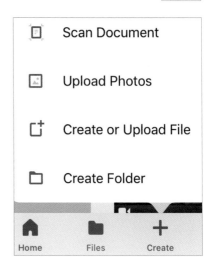

5 To copy an item to Dropbox from your iPad, such as a photo, open it in its own app, select it, and tap on the **Share** button

6 Select the Dropbox option (in some apps this may have to be accessed from the **More** button on the Share menu)

iPad for Presentations

Just as you would use your laptop to present your PowerPoint or Keynote slides, you can use your iPad by hooking it up to an AV projector or screen.

You will need to buy a Lightning to VGA Adapter. This plugs in to the bottom of the iPad, and the other end connects to the VGA projector.

Present using an AV projector

 **Connect** the iPad to the projector using the Lightning to VGA Adapter

 Open **Keynote**

3 Choose **Presentation**

The file will open in Presentation mode (rather than Edit mode).

The iPad is great for giving presentations, and saves you having to drag a heavy laptop around!

If you have access to an HD display you would be better using the HDMI connector (Lightning Digital AV Adapter).

Printing from the iPad

The iPad supports wireless printing, using its in-built technology called **AirPrint**. This can be used with a compatible AirPrint printer. Apple has provided support for many printers, and a full list can be found at **https://support.apple.com/kb/HT4356**

Once an AirPrint printer has been set up it can then be used to print wirelessly from your iPad:

Hot tip

To use an AirPrint printer, it has to first be connected to your Wi-Fi network, This can be done through **Settings** > **Wi-Fi** and selecting the printer name, or it can be done through the printer's own control panel. Check the printer's documentation for details.

1. For most apps, tap on the **Share** button

2. Tap on the **Print** button

3. Tap on the **Select Printer** option

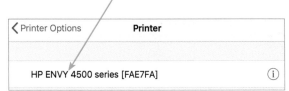

4. Tap on the required AirPrint printer

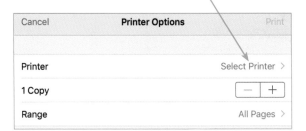

5. Select options for the print job, such as number of pages and color options, and tap on **Print**

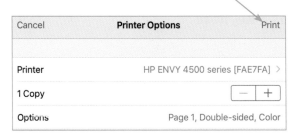

18 Accessibility Options

The iPad has some very effective adjustments, which make it easy to use for people with visual and other impairments. This chapter highlights the main accessibility settings that will make the iPad work for you even if you have sight or auditory issues.

Accessibility

The iPad tries to cater to as wide a range of users as possible, including those who have difficulty with vision or hearing, or have physical and motor issues. There are a number of settings that can help with these areas. To access the range of accessibility settings:

1 Open the **Settings** app and select **General** > **Accessibility**

2 The settings for **Vision**, **Interaction**, **Hearing**, **Media** and **Learning** are displayed here

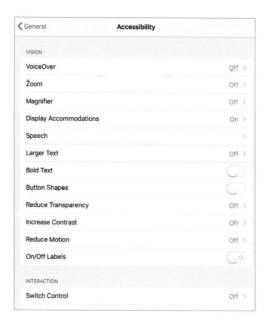

3 Tap on a main category to view the options within it

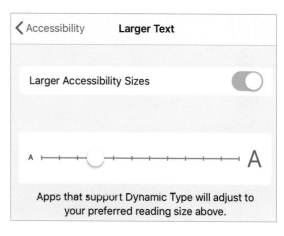

VoiceOver

This setting enables the iPad to tell you what's on the screen, even if you cannot see the screen.

1 Touch the screen or drag your fingers to hear the screen items described

2 If text is selected, VoiceOver will read the text to you

To turn VoiceOver On

1 Go to **Settings** > **General** > **Accessibility** > **VoiceOver**

2 Tap **VoiceOver** to turn On or Off

3 Tap **Speak Hints** On or Off

VoiceOver gestures

Tap	Speak item
Flick Left or Right	Select next or previous item
Flick Up or Down	Depends on Rotor Control setting
Two-finger Tap	Stop speaking current selection
Two-finger Flick Up	Read all from top of screen
Two-finger Flick Down	Read all from current position
Three-finger Flick Up/Down	Scroll one page at a time
Three-finger Flick Left/Right	Next or previous page
Three-finger Tap	Speak the scroll status
Four-finger Flick Up/Down	Go to first or last element on page
Four-finger Flick Left/Right	Next or previous section

If you cannot see the screen text, VoiceOver will read it to you.

VoiceOver works with the pre-installed iPad apps and some apps from the App Store, but not all of them.

Accessibility Features

There are numerous other accessibility features that can be deployed on the iPad. These can all be accessed from **Settings** > **General** > **Accessibility**:

Vision

The Vision options include the following:

- **VoiceOver**. (See page 231.)

- **Zoom**. This can be used to increase and decrease the screen magnification. Double-tap the screen with three fingers to increase the magnification by 200%. Double-tap with three fingers again to return it to the original size. Drag with three fingers to move around the screen.

- **Magnifier**. This can be used to turn on the Magnifier, which uses the iPad's camera to magnify what it is viewing. Triple-click the Home button to activate it.

- **Display Accommodations**. This can apply settings to the iPad's display, such as inverting screen colors and applying color filters.

- **Speech**. This can be used to determine options for spoken items on the iPad.

- **Larger Text**. Use this to allow compatible apps to increase the size of text.

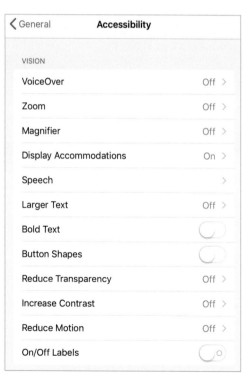

‹ General	Accessibility	
VISION		
VoiceOver	Off ›	
Zoom	Off ›	
Magnifier	Off ›	
Display Accommodations	On ›	
Speech	›	
Larger Text	Off ›	
Bold Text		
Button Shapes		
Reduce Transparency	Off ›	
Increase Contrast	Off ›	
Reduce Motion	Off ›	
On/Off Labels		

- **Bold Text**. This can be turned On to create bold text on the iPad. It requires a restart to apply it.

...cont'd

- **Button Shapes**. Turn this On to underline buttons.

- **Reduce Transparency**. This can be used to improve screen contrast and increase legibility of text.

- **Increase Contrast**. This aids legibility by increasing the contrast with some backgrounds.

- **Reduce Motion**. This reduces the amount of motion effects that are applied throughout the iPad.

- **On/Off Labels**. This defines the On/Off buttons further by adding labels to them as well as their standard colors.

Hearing
The Hearing options include the following:

- **MFi Hearing Devices**. This can be used to set up a range of hearing devices to be used with the iPad.

- **LED Flash for Alerts**. This causes the screen to flash when an alert or specified notification is received.

- **Mono Audio**. Instead of stereo sound, Mono Audio channels both right and left output into a single mono output. This is useful for people with a hearing impairment, since they can hear the output from both channels in one ear. Turn Mono Audio On and Off.

Media
The Media options include the following:

- **Subtitles and Captioning**. This determines the style of captions and subtitles on the iPad, if used.

- **Audio Descriptions**. If this is On, audio descriptions will automatically play, where they are available.

Learning
The Learning options are:

- **Guided Access**. The Guided Access option allows for certain functionalities within an app to be disabled so that individual tasks can be focused on without any other distractions. For instance, areas of a web page can be disabled so that the page being viewed cannot be moved away from.

The **Hearing** options also include **Hearing Aid Compatibility**, which can be used to improve audio quality for some hearing aids.

233

When you first activate Guided Access for an app you will need to enter a passcode. This must also be entered when you leave Guided Access.

...cont'd

● **Accessibility Shortcut**. These are settings for selecting options for the functions that are activated by triple-clicking the Home button.

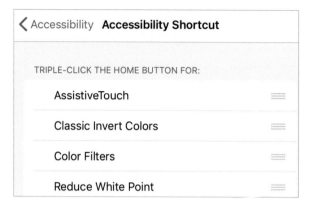

Interaction
The Interaction options include the following:

● **Switch Control**. This can be used to set up your iPad for an adaptive accessory such as a mouse, keyboard, or joystick.

● **AssistiveTouch**. This contains a range of options that reduce the need for using your hands and fingers as much as for standard use.

● **Touch Accommodations.** This can be used to change how the screen responds to touch.

● **Home Button**. This can be used to adjust the speed for double-clicking and triple-clicking the Home button.

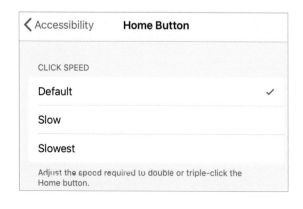

The **AssistiveTouch** options make it easier for anyone with difficulties clicking the Home button, or using gestures.

By default, **Shake to Undo** is enabled so that you can shake the iPad to undo the most recent action. However, this can be turned off within the Interaction section, so that actions are not undone if you shake your iPad by accident.

Index

D

E

F

G

H

I

K

T

V

W